Report of a Joint Working Party on

HEALTH NEEDS OF SCHOOL AGE CHILDREN

Chaired by
Leon Polnay

September 1995

Published by

British Paediatric Association

British Paediatric Association
5 St Andrews Place
Regent's Park
London NW1 4LB

Tel: 0171 486 6151 Fax: 0171 486 6009

Registered Charity No. 285235

British Paediatric Association, 5 St Andrews Place, Regent's Park, London NW1 4LB UK.

ISBN 0 9500491 9 0

Editorial and production: Sundara (Sam) Lingam, honorary assistant editor, BPA

Technical assistant: Philippa Davies, publications dept., BPA

Index: Nina Boyd

Design and typesetting: Mehmet Hussein

Printed in Great Britain by Freedman Brothers (Printers) Ltd, London

Foreword

by

Roy Meadow
President, BPA

Because so much of the acute illness of childhood occurs in the very young, there has been a tendency to give the health needs of school children a lesser priority. Yet none doubt that the best investment in the country's future is in its children. Although the key targets of *Health of the Nation* mainly concern adults, most adult problems have their origins in childhood and many can be prevented by ensuring the optimal health of children. Just as the skills of the nation depend on the education of children, so the health of the nation follows from the physical and mental health of its children.

The report emphasises the services that are necessary for children at school, in the setting of the adjacent general medical care (primary care) and hospital care (secondary care). The composition of the working party chaired by Dr Leon Polnay, an experienced community paediatrician, reflects some of the diversity in the delivery of healthcare to children - paediatric specialists, general practitioners, public health doctors and community health nurses. These health professionals stress the importance of working closely with other agencies, and in partnership with children, teachers and parents. At a time when there is emphasis on empowering parents to act on behalf of children, there is also a recognition that many parents need positive guidance and directive advice.

Contents

Information

Good information at a locality level is a key requirement for child health services for the school age child. This information should be used in an annual report to the governors of individual schools and the Director of Public Health. The report should review the health of the school population and include recommendations on unmet needs. A district *factfile* should be compiled to aid this process.

Named responsibility

Certain key tasks require named paediatric and nursing responsibility from specialised professionals. These include named persons for child protection; immunisation; 1993 Education Act advice; children *looked after* and adolescent health.

A service for all children

Programmes of care covering health promotion, accident prevention, child health surveillance, dental health and adolescent health are recommended for all school children whether in independent or maintained schools. These are key programmes to promote health, identify ill health and ensure that secondary services are appropriately targeted, thus reducing the impact of health problems on educational progress.

The school nurse is the main focus point for the whole school population. Selective referral to the school paediatrician will follow school nurse health appraisal. This will not lead to reduction in workload, but needs will be more effectively targeted.

Doctors and nurses working in schools require privacy and a suitable environment for interviews and examinations.

The service to schools should have a high profile and be easily accessed by pupils, parents and teachers.

School children are an important group with regard to Health of the Nation targets. Examples are in accident prevention, sex education, smoking and mental health. Innovative health promotion programmes should be developed and those in place should be evaluated.

Children in need

Health Authorities have statutory duties under the 1989 Children Act to identify and provide services to children in need. Children in need, (including children with special educational needs), require services from education and social services as well as the primary, secondary and tertiary elements of health services. We recommend the close co-operation of all of these services in the spirit of the 1989 Children Act and that the health components of this operate a seamless service. For educational medicine, the child development centre should work closely with schools and locality clinics.

Emotional and behavioural problems are the largest cause of disability among children of school age. Districts should have a programme for mental health promotion as well as one for referral and treatment.

General paediatric referral clinics in the community can provide a locally sensitive service and, if not already in place, should be established.

Policies for the management of children with critical illness both at home and at school should be developed in each district.

Child protection programmes should be comprehensive, requiring a strategy for prevention as well as programmes for identification, investigation and management.

Children *looked after* are an important group of children in need with, in general, poor health, mental health and educational outcomes. We recommend that districts develop a customised programme of care for them.

Disadvantaged children have poorer health than the general population. We recommend that they are identified through health services to schools and that this is used to target resources on the areas of greatest need.

Manpower and training

Every school requires a named nurse and paediatrician with special training in the health of children and young people and in educational medicine. In addition to the named responsibility noted above, doctors and nurses who fill these specialist roles should have received the appropriate specialist training. We recommend that very high priority be given to training and continuing education as the recognised engine that drives a quality service; it should be included in contracts. Training should include a strong interdisciplinary element in line with the shape of service envisaged in this report.

Research and development

We recommend a research portfolio with specific areas to be addressed in the health of the school age child. The academic base of the subject. should be expanded and established in every medical school.

Technical reports providing benchmarks for services are required in the following areas: assessment and management of children with developmental problems; mental health problems in children in residential schools, children *looked after*, children excluded from school or following abuse or neglect; investigation of child abuse and neglect; health needs assessment of children *looked after*; models of good practice for inner city areas.

Medication in schools

There is an urgent need for clear and authoritative guidelines on giving medication to children at school. We recommend that an expert medical, nursing, education and legal group is established to provide these.

Independent schools

We recommend all school children should receive the same programmes of care, including those who attend independent schools. We recommend that a working group is established with the Medical Officers of Schools Association and representatives of the Independent Schools Joint Council to make recommendations on how this may be achieved.

1
Introduction

This report was commissioned by the BPA with the remit *to review the health needs of school age children and how they may be met.* The report centres around the comprehensive programmes of care, which interface with education.

The health service for school age children, as discussed in this report, is a specialist service whose unique feature is the application of our knowledge about health and illness in an educational setting. It includes among its tasks the monitoring and promotion of health in school children (primary prevention); the identification of ill health, disability, and problems of development or behaviour so that they are understood and appropriately managed, thus avoiding or minimising consequential learning difficulties, (secondary and tertiary prevention); and the recognition of the contribution of social factors in understanding children's well-being. The twin focuses of the service are the individual and the whole population of school age children.

This report has been prepared following the publication of a consultation document with this title published in December 1993. Over 100 individuals and organisations responded and it is hoped that this new report reflects the views expressed. Most of the advice received was constructive and positive. Whilst it was possible to simply revise the original document, we felt that so much had changed in the short time between December 1993 and the end of the consultation process in June 1994, that it would be better to produce an entirely new document. Important events taking place over that time were the publication of the 1993 Education Act, the Audit Commission report, *Seen but not Heard,* and the introduction of changes in the career structure and training for doctors in community child health. The Audit Commission concluded in their consideration of school health that, *"there appears to be a lack of clarity over service objectives and outcomes, with insufficient collaboration between professionals providing services".*

This report was needed as there has been no comprehensive review of community child health services for school age children since the Court Report in 1976. Many of the recommendations of the Court Report have been implemented including the appointment of consultant paediatricians in community child health and the establishment of district handicap teams, though not yet in every district. The service has changed in many ways with moves towards a more specialist service, training programmes are in place for community paediatricians and new national policies incorporated in the

Children Act 1989, *the Health of the Nation* (1992) and the Education Act 1993. The health of adolescents has been of particular concern and is highlighted in the Chief Medical Officer's report for 1993. There is evidence of deterioration in some measures of health with an increase in reported chronic illness and widespread evidence of increasingly unhealthy lifestyles. The General Household Survey reported a doubling in the prevalence of chronic illness from 1972 to 1991, (much of which is accounted for by an increase in asthma); the suicide rate for young men age 15-19 has almost doubled since the mid-1970s; obesity is increasing in the same age group and schoolchildren consume too much fat in their diets; teenage conceptions increased in the ten year period until 1991 when a small drop was observed.

Some purchasers are uncertain of the role of community child health services in this new environment, especially for those services that are provided for children at school. The aim of this report is to clarify this role with the needs of purchasers in mind. Throughout this report we use the term "health needs of school age children" rather than "school health services" because we wish to emphasise the position of this service as closely linked to all other specialist paediatric services.

We are aware, through our work in preparing this report and through the experience of other working parties devoted to child health surveillance for the pre-school child and the personal child health record, that there is no such thing as a "definitive report". The best a working party can do is to analyse the available evidence and be prepared to modify this in future publications in the light of new research and experience gained from implementation of the proposals. We expect, therefore, a comparatively short shelf life as has been the case for these other publications.

This report covers a very broad range of services and programmes of care. It is intended to provide "signposts". Detailed directions for clinicians will require a related series of technical reports and it is hoped that these will be commissioned to follow on from this publication.

This report makes no recommendations for hospital paediatric care or for the comprehensive arrangements for general medical services that are provided by primary health care teams, but does highlight the necessity for communication and liaison in order to provide the aimed for seamless service.

Collaborative working is a cornerstone of the health services for children of school age. Contracts should include within them the requirement and the time for interdisciplinary and inter-agency communication. In particular we recommend the development of district consortia for particular programmes of care, strong local networks with education and social services and agreed local protocols for referral and management with general practitioners.

2

Definitions

Age limits

The report covers children of compulsory school age between five and sixteen years. It emphasises the need for liaison with general practitioners in relation to pre-school child health surveillance and school leavers.

Health

Within the term we include child development, physical and mental health, and health promotion.

Paediatrician

Throughout this report the term paediatrician is used to describe all doctors working in the child health services as recommended and agreed by an *ad hoc* working party convened by the BPA on 22 March 1994.

Primary care

This describes the services that are available for and are intended to be delivered to all children and to which they can refer themselves directly. It includes services provided through the primary health care team, child health surveillance and health promotion.

Secondary care

This describes the specialist services that are required by some children. They are accessed by referral and include community services for children in need, community referral clinics and hospital paediatric services.

Public health medicine

This describes the branch of medicine concerned with the monitoring and promotion of health of the whole population in contrast to individual health care. This includes assessment of the health needs of the population.

Community child health services developed through public health services at the beginning of this century. It can still be regarded as a public health programme in its application to the whole school population, its role in identification of ill health, (as well as management), and its involvement in monitoring and promoting health.

3

Background and History

The school health services were established in the UK following the publication of the *1904 Report of the Interdepartmental Committee on Physical Deterioration.* This report was produced in response to the high rate of rejection of recruits during the Boer War. The report recognised the importance of health in childhood as a pre-requisite for health in adult life. Its 53 recommendations included advice on anthropometric survey; overcrowding; buildings and open spaces; air pollution; alcoholism; juvenile smoking; food and cooking; adulteration of foods; physical exercise; and medical inspection of school children. As a consequence of the report, school nurses and doctors were appointed to meet some of these important health needs.

The report and its recommendations were firmly based on the promotion of health and many parallel those of *Health of the Nation, 1992* nearly 90 years later.

The 1904 Report led to the passing of the 1907 Education Act which marked the beginnings of a universal school health service. This service was established long before most cities had dedicated hospital services for children, the advent of the National Health Service and the universal availability of GP led primary care services. The emphasis was on the promotion of health as well as providing treatment and a growing role in the provision of advice to the local authority. The 1944 Education Act gave local authorities the duty to provide medical and dental inspection and treatment in all types of maintained schools, and to ascertain children needing special education. The 1974 NHS Act, transferred responsibility for school health services from the local authority to the district health authority (DHA). Since 1977, the DHA has been responsible for the purchase of health services for school children, but nowhere are standards or objectives for these services set down.

The Education Acts 1981 and 1993 require health authorities to notify the education authority of children likely to have special educational needs and to submit a medical report of advice as part of the statement of special educational needs. It places emphasis on multidisciplinary assessment, involvement of parents, and greater integration of children with special needs within mainstream schools. A named doctor is responsible for co-ordinating advice to the education authority. In the 1993 legislation, medical reports must be submitted within six weeks of the request if the child is already known to the service.

The 1989 Children Act unifies much of the legislation related to children and provides a framework in which health, education and social services could work more closely together. It requires social service departments, in collaboration with health authorities, to identify children in need - including children with disabilities and, as appropriate, provide support to these children and their families. It also requires inspection of independent boarding schools by the local authority. The Act includes collaborative arrangements with regard to child protection, children *looked after,* children with disabilities and other children categorised as "in need".

The Health of the Nation Report, 1992, provides important challenges and targets for improved health. Many of the individual recommendations are strikingly similar to those of the 1904 report which led to the setting up of a universal school health service. The current services are uniquely placed to play a leading role in the development of strategies to meet *Health of the Nation* targets. The five key target areas are coronary heart disease and stroke; cancers; mental illness; HIV/AIDS and sexual health; accidents. These provide major tasks for the health service in important areas such as childhood nutrition, smoking, exercise, reduction of teenage pregnancy, reduction of sexually transmitted diseases, reduction in childhood accidents with specific targets for children and young people; reduction in suicide; alcohol and drug misuse.

The UN Convention on the Rights of the Child, (ratified by the UK parliament), recognises the right of a child with a handicap to special care, education and training designed to lead to the achievement of the greatest possible self reliance and a full and active life in society, (article 23). Article 24 recognises the right of children to the highest level of health possible and to access to health and medical services, with special emphasis on primary and preventive health care, public health education and the reduction of infant mortality. Article 16 concerns the right to privacy and confidentiality. Article 3.1 states that the children's best interests are a primary consideration in any decision which may affect them either as individuals or as a group. Article 12 concerns the right of children to express their own views about their health and treatment or about the provision of services which might affect them and have them taken into account according to the age and maturity of the child.

Northern Ireland

There has been a school health service in Northern Ireland since the early 1900s. The Public Health (Medical Treatment of Children) (Ireland) Act 1919 made particular provision for the medical inspection and treatment of children attending school. The Education Act (Northern Ireland) 1923 made similar provisions, placing an obligation on the education authority to provide for the medical and dental inspection of children in schools under the management of, or aided by, the education authority. The Public Health and Local Government (Transfer of Functions) (No 2) Order (Northern Ireland) 1948 transferred these responsibilities from the education authority to the health authority. The Health and Personal Social Services (Northern Ireland) Order 1972 currently requires the health and social services board to provide for the medical and dental supervision and periodic inspection of grant aided school pupils. Separate provision may be made in voluntary grammar schools by means of an approved scheme. Boards may also arrange for the supervision and inspection of pupils attending independent schools. The Education and Libraries (Northern Ireland) Order 1986 requires grant aided schools to provide facilities to enable the school health service to carry out its duties. Under the Order, responsibility for assessing the special educational needs of school children rests with the education and library boards. The Education (Special Educational Needs) Regulations (Northern Ireland) 1985 require the education and library boards to consult the appropriate health board when making an assessment or re-assessment or when preparing a statement of a child's special educational needs. In Northern Ireland health targets have been set since 1987. The report, *A Regional Strategy for the Northern Ireland Health and Personal Social Services 1992-97,* sets objectives and targets.

Scotland

In Scotland, the medical and dental inspection of all children continues to be a statutory requirement under the National Health Service (Scotland) Act 1978. The equivalent to the 1981 Education Act in Scotland is the Education (Scotland) Act 1980 (as amended). The Children Act 1989, for the most part does not apply in Scotland. The parallel document to *Health of the Nation* is, *Scotland's Health: A Challenge to us All.* There is no national curriculum in Scotland, with responsibility lying with education authorities and head teachers. Guidance is, however, given by the Scottish Examination Board and the Scottish Vocational Education Council, with National Guidelines on Environmental Studies 5-14 and Personal and Social Development 5-14. These will be fully in place by 1999 and emphasise the need for a whole school approach to healthy and safe living.

Wales

The Strategic Intent and Direction for Wales was launched in 1989. The Welsh Health Planning Forum has published ***Protocols for Investment in Health Gain*** which identifies health gain opportunities for children.

3.1 Aims and objectives for health services for school age children

(Modified from, *Community Child Health Services: An Information Base for Purchasers,* BPA,1992)

Aims

- To achieve the best possible level of health (mental and physical) and social well being, current and future for all children of school age;
- Working in partnership with children, parents and teachers to enable children to benefit fully from education.

Objectives

To work in collaboration with other professionals, parents and children to meet the following objectives:

- To ensure that children are encouraged and enabled to take responsibility for their own health and to adopt a healthy lifestyle, leading to:

  -an increase in:
    * positive health behaviour;
    * confidence and self esteem;
    * parenting skills of the next generation.

  -a decrease in:
    * psychological ill health in families;
    * child abuse in future generations.

- To reduce social inequalities in health by:
    * targeting of resources;
    * improving access to services;
    * improving parenting skills.

- To decrease preventable causes of ill health and disability:
    - accidents, infection, substance abuse, smoking, alcohol, sexually transmitted disease.

- To support teachers in the delivery of health education programmes for their pupils;

- To complement primary care services in the early detection and management of ill health in this age group;

- To minimise the effects of common childhood disabilities and major health problems upon daily living, school life and education and to ensure that all children are able to derive maximum benefit from the education offered to them;

- To provide advice on health issues to children and parents, teachers, education welfare officers, careers' officers and the Local Education Authority.

4

Changing Context of Health Services for School Age Children

Much of the pressure for reform in the school health service originates from the perception of changing needs of the population and in the organisation, role and responsibilities of the health, education and social services. This section of the report summarises the principal changes perceived to have taken place in the population served by the community child health services and in other services for children and their families.

4.1 The family

The present population trend is one of increasing divorce rate, with the UK rate the highest in the European Union. Research has demonstrated family discord to be related to emotional distress and behavioural disturbance expressed by children and young people. The number of single parent families is rising, (30% of births outside marriage), and these figures include worrying numbers of very young mothers who experience teenage pregnancies, separated lone parents and unemployed single mothers, supported by state benefits.

Population mobility, sometimes to meet housing or employment demands, has resulted in a loss of intergenerational support available to larger and extended families, where members remain not only close but in proximity. There is a continuing rise in the number of employed women including those in part-time work, necessitating a variety of child care arrangements to meet needs. In extreme cases children have been left alone. Remarriages result in reconstituted families and step parenting which brings its own stresses as well as rewards and opportunities.

There have been significant and quite rapid changes in family patterns in the population which have resulted in major shifts in the experience children now have of family life and of child care patterns and support. Culture and lifestyles have changed considerably, for example in terms of increased car ownership and changes from walking to school to being driven to school; changes in diet and eating patterns (fast foods etc.).

The outcome of these family experiences, when they prove negative, may present as major stress, psychological difficulties, poor school attainment, conduct disorders, (including confrontation with the law), and poor adjustment for significant numbers of children. These features often continue into adult life and result in a cycle of disadvantage with similar difficulties appearing in the next generation.

4.2 The community

The community is changing and developing in new ways as a collection of families, in the physical environment and in its cultural diversity. Concern has been expressed at the limitations of some freedoms, (for example independent travel to school), now enjoyed by children compared with those a generation or two ago, such that the development of independence skills may be impaired.

There are material changes in society, with significant numbers suffering poverty and disadvantage and evidence that inequality in the distribution of wealth has increased over the last fifteen years, with the poor becoming poorer. The amenities available to children and their families, (and their expectation in relation to resources available, as well as inequalities in the distribution of wealth), are additional factors reported to contribute to stress and inequalities in health. There is evidence that homelessness in young people and families with young children, as well as those in temporary accommodation, may add significantly to the burden upon health care for the wellbeing, health and development in a significant number of children.

Opportunities for employment for young people leaving school, the effects of unemployment upon families, the stability and security of employment enjoyed by those in work and the requirement to develop new or changing skills to meet changing employment needs, may all alter traditional patterns of family and working life and place new stresses upon children and their parents.

As society becomes more multicultural there are greater differences in customs, religion, dress and language, with threats to some arising from racism and discrimination. For others, there are tensions suffered as the children and young people integrate faster than their family of origin. These young people have to cope with conflicting expectations between their family and peer group.

4.3 Changes in child health in the UK

Infant and later childhood mortality have both fallen. Rather less is known about morbidity; there is reported evidence of an increase in the prevalence of asthma. Epilepsy is now well controlled in the majority, but for a few there are major challenges to the achievement of a satisfactory quality of life. There are gratifying improved survival rates in very low birth weight babies. Many will achieve normal health and development, but a proportion of survivors suffer disability, have special educational needs, and other less apparent learning difficulties, such as perceptuomotor problems, that are identified later in their school life.

The 1988 study of disability in childhood carried out by OPCS revealed a prevalence of disabilities likely to have a significant effect on carrying out everyday activities in 3.5% of 10-15 year-olds. Greatest numbers, (in descending order of prevalence), were found in the categories of behaviour, communication, continence, locomotion, intellectual functioning, personal care and hearing.

There are changes in health related behaviour, with an increase in teenage conceptions until the most recent year for which figures are available (1991), when a small fall was seen, and rising use of alcohol as well as misuse of tobacco and drugs. Concern about poor diet and lack of regular exercise place these children at increased risk of heart disease in adult life. These concerns are voiced in the government's *Health of the Nation* White Paper and are reflected in the targets set.

The improvement in immunisation uptake has resulted in a reduction in deaths and disabilities due to infectious disease and its sequelae. However new epidemics of familiar diseases may still threaten, for example measles and rubella.

The overall prevalence of dental decay is declining. However, in certain groups of children, deprived children and children from ethnic minorities, dental decay is static or increasing.

These changes in child health, (as well as in the background to health described under the family and the community), present very vividly the health needs of the school age group, highlighting the level of disability particularly in areas likely to have important effects upon learning, the burden of emotional and behaviour problems and the pressing need for effective health promotion. These areas should be identified as major tasks for the health services for children of school age.

4.4 Changes in the health service

Health Authorities, Health Boards, District Heath Authorities, Family Health Service Authorities

4.4.1 Purchaser/provider

Under the new arrangements, health authorities and boards and other purchasers, including GP fundholders, act as commissioning authorities, while directly managed units (DMUs) and trusts act as providers of services. It is part of the public health medicine responsibility to formulate, monitor and implement the health authority policies. Purchasers need to ascertain what services **must** be provided and to consider cooperative arrangements between agencies. Priorities must be set and difficult judgements made on the need and effectiveness of different types of service. Guidance is given in the BPA publication, *Community Child Health Services: An Information Base for Purchasers, (1992).*

4.4.2 Combined child health service

The concept of the combined child health service has been advocated by the BPA in its 1991 report *Towards a Combined Child Health Service.* In this model, hospital and community services are combined and managed together. It has been widely supported but progress has been slow in implementation, especially where hospital and community services are in different trusts. Others have feared that within such a combined service there would be inequality in the importance attached to community compared with hospital services, to the disadvantage of the former. A compromise has been to commission services that are combined at the point of delivery.

4.4.3 General medical services

Although many family doctors are providing a child health surveillance programme for pre-school children, health services provided for children within school are not part of general medical services for this age group, ie from 5 years until 16. They are not included within the regulations for child health surveillance by family doctors. These services are also not included in fundholding regulations. Liaison between the preschool and school age services is essential, as well as a continuing dialogue between specialist community paediatric services and primary health care teams on current health issues and for school leavers with special needs. Liaison can take place through regular meetings with school nurse or doctor, correspondence, or through referral clinics held on GP premises. Some children, especially in inner city areas, may not be registered with a family doctor and school health services can provide an important safety net for this group. However, paediatricians in community child health should make every effort to encourage children and their families to register with a general practitioner, rather than attempt to provide a substitute primary care service.

4.4.4 School nursing developments and training

School nurses are all registered general nurses, some of whom will also be registered sick children's nurses and some will also have completed a post-registration specialist school nursing course at a college of higher education or a university. The school nurse is the key figure in ensuring effective communication between school based services and primary health care teams, teachers, parents and other health professionals. She is also a source of information about local health services for the school community. Within a team of school nurses there is a need for a variety of skills, for example in health promotion, or work with teenagers or children with severe disabilities. Professional leadership and a career structure that permits individual development and advancement are both required.

Training programmes are now in place for school nursing but there is patchy access and uptake across the country. The expanded role in health promotion, surveillance and management described in this report requires a comprehensive training for all. Improvements in training, on a par with health visiting and district nursing, will result from programmes planned by the UKCC for community health nursing. Training should include the core curriculum for all post-registration community nurses as outlined by the National Boards for Nursing, Midwifery and Health Visiting with stated specific learning outcomes in clinical nursing practice and care and programme management for children at school. In addition, continuing post-registration education will be required as it will for all nurses. Changes in preregistration training of nurses, (Project 2000), will also yield benefits in the final level of qualification achieved by school nurses and the service delivered by them.

4.4.5 A consultant-led community paediatric service

Following the recommendations of the Court Report in 1976, consultant paediatricians in community child health have increasingly been trained and appointed to provide professional leadership to paediatricians working in the community. Training posts at senior house officer, registrar and senior registrar levels have been established. In 1992, 201 consultants had been appointed, with 44 senior registrars and 19 registrars, (BPA Manpower survey). Clinical medical officer and senior clinical medical officer posts will be gradually replaced with appointments as staff grade and associate specialist posts as part of the unification of the career structure for doctors, *(Report on Medical Services for Children, 1992).* There are opportunities for regrading of current clinical and senior clinical medical officers to staff grade, associate specialist or consultant appointments. Each of the two new grades will have a recommended training programme. These two career level posts ensure essential expertise and continuity of care that cannot be provided by doctors in rotating training posts. Appointments to consultant paediatric posts are difficult to make at present, because of the shortage of trainees, with some posts remaining vacant. The *Report of the Working Group on Specialist Medical Training, (1993),* will introduce a shorter and more focused period of higher professional training. Sufficient posts must be established to meet all of these training needs. In addition plans for continuing medical education, (CME), for all paediatricians are being prepared by the BPA. Undergraduate teaching of community paediatrics should also be highlighted and expanded. All of these educational developments should be based upon sound research and clinical practice. MSc courses, on a part time or full time basis, have a growing role in the training of community paediatricians in addition to the college based qualifications of MRCP, DCH and DCCH.

4.4.6 Child and adolescent psychiatry

Behaviour problems emerged as the commonest cause of disability in childhood in the OPCS survey. In spite of this, many districts find that service provision falls far short of service needs with actual reduction of service and staffing being reported by some (Kurtz 1994). Examples are 15% of districts with fewer than one child and adolescent psychiatrist; three quarters of schools for children with emotional and behavioural difficulties report inadequate support for pupils' mental health needs. There is a continuum of service needs from those less severe problems that are usually managed by paediatricians to extremely severe and complex problems that require highly specialised units for their management. Some districts do not have sufficient clinical psychologists as well as child psychiatrists and psychologists to work with child development teams. There is a need to ensure that paediatricians are adequately trained in the management of the less complex and severe behaviour problems and that districts, as a whole, are able to purchase services for the whole range of presenting emotional and behavioural problems.

4.4.7 Therapy services

These are an essential component for the assessment and management of services for children with special educational needs. Speech and language therapists, paediatric physiotherapists and occupational therapists are required to contribute to the service for children in mainstream and special schools as well as in the clinic and home.

4.4.8 Management of child health services

Management of community child health services has changed greatly. Posts of specialist in community medicine (child health), have been gradually replaced since the 1982 reorganisation abolishing area health authorities. Increasingly, consultant paediatricians in community child health and then clinical directors, specialty managers and others were appointed. Professional management within a discipline needs to be distinguished from the overall management of a service provided by many disciplines. The co-ordination of the "team" that provides services to a locality or a family of schools is often not straightforward as the various members of that team, (nurses, therapists, doctors), usually have separate managers and form an *"Association Network"* (Øvretveit, 1993).

Health services for school children require local co-ordination of the various workforces involved, common policies and protocols and recognised leadership with responsibility and authority to bind the professionally and geographically separate elements into an effective service.

4.4.9 Fruits of research

The academic development of community paediatrics and school nursing has led to an expansion of research and this has led to changes in practice. Examples are to be found in child health surveillance, school profiling, immunisation, health promotion, accident prevention and infant nutrition. However, much more research and development is needed across the whole range of disciplines involved in school health. This will give a more secure basis to the individual elements of many of the programmes of care.

There is great scope for research contributions from academics and practitioners in nursing and social science as well as in paediatric epidemiology, and from research and development programmes, clinical audit and evaluative studies in school health.

4.4.10 Changes in professional and service roles

The last ten to twenty years have seen large changes in the professional roles taken within community child health services, but with widely differing states of development between districts. The repetitive routine examinations by doctors have been abandoned, though some still retain this at school entry. School nurses have expanded their role in health appraisal and health education and emerged as the key profession for the whole school population. Paediatricians working in schools are increasingly providing a specialist paediatric service for individuals, though retaining a population overview. Liaison with family doctors, who now provide the bulk of preschool child health surveillance, has greatly improved. Some secondary services, previously provided in hospital, especially child protection, services for children with disabilities, and some general paediatrics, are increasingly delivered by paediatricians working in the community. The Audit Commission in its publication *Seen but not Heard, 1994* found large variations in staffing between districts; these probably reflect the varying stages they have reached in the reallocation of professional roles and the development of the service into new models.

4.4.11 Training

Training programmes have already been mentioned for school nurses and paediatricians. The weakness of the service has often been seen in the lack of specialty training in comparison with other groups of nurses and doctors. Training has been a driving force behind developments in the service, but needs to be expanded much further if the potential of the service and the expectations of purchasers and parents are to be met. Every medical school should be able to offer undergraduate and postgraduate training in this specialty.

4.5 Local authorities

4.5.1 The social services

Effects of the Children Act 1989

The Children Act 1989 placed new and broad duties upon social services for *children in need*. The new role is proactive as well as reactive. The implementation of the Act has been against a background of reduction in expenditure in many authorities. Local re-organisations of social service departments have taken place to reflect the requirements of the Children Act. A key theme of the Act is to increase collaboration between health, education and social services for *children in need*. However the 1993/94 survey by the RCN, *Nursing and Child Protection* found that 49% of DHAs/ Boards did not have systematic population data on *children in need* within their area.

Social services department responsibilities for children include identification of *children in need;* support of families with *children in need;* to publish information about the services they provide; to prevent abuse and neglect; to provide accommodation, (children *looked after);* to provide assessment and review for children *looked after,* including a health care plan; and to provide aftercare for young people who have left the care system.

4.5.2 The Local Education Authority, (Education and Library Boards in Northern Ireland)

Local management of schools, (LMS), has given individual schools much greater autonomy in managing their own affairs and budgets. Whilst this may give them freedom to decide priorities, there is a risk that the need for some activities, such as health promotion may go unrecognised or be given low priority or resource allocation within the school. Schools require expert medical and nursing advice.

More children with special needs are being educated in mainstream schools, as recommended in the 1981 and 1993 Education Acts, rather than being concentrated in special schools. The placing of special needs children in most, if not all, mainstream school has lead to increased complexity in organisation and in the distribution of school health specialist services and special education resources to all schools.

Health education is included in the national curriculum. Restrictions in the 1993 Education Act in teaching on sex education and in teachers' freedom to give individual advice to pupils have caused widespread concern among health workers and some tensions. Some see this as a barrier to collaboration in sex education and achieving Health of the Nation targets of reduction in teenage pregnancies and sexually transmitted diseases.

Changes in the inspectorate will require new arrangements to ensure that health and education services continue to work together. Loss of health education advisers and specialised central teaching teams will also require major adjustments to be made in the way services are delivered. Local education psychology services will continue to be provided by the LEA.

The "moderating groups" to be established under the 1993 Education Act are designed as a forum to develop agreed local interpretation of guidance.

4.6 Independent schools

The health needs of children in day and boarding independent schools have largely fallen outside the remit of community paediatricians and nurses.

Provision has varied very widely but, in general, national recommendations have not been applied. In some parts of the country, 25% of pupils attend independent schools. There is a growing body of opinion that there should be equity in school health provision for all children. Independent schools which admit children with special needs require the same specialist paediatric services as maintained schools.

Inspection of boarding schools by the local authority is now required by the Children Act 1989. This requirement reflects the recognition of the isolation and vulnerability of children within residential education.

4.7 Non-statutory organisations

These organisations are an important part of service provision. They may provide resources, information or support and may be included in contracts as may independent schools. Examples of these agencies are NSPCC, BDA and RNIB. Voluntary organisations are often able to provide services and an understanding which many parents cannot find from the statutory agencies. Collaboration between voluntary and statutory bodies greatly enhances the effectiveness of the service network.

Meeting Needs - Principles and Frameworks

5.1 General principles

- Children should be seen as children first and require to be seen in a setting and with an approach which reflects this.

- Each child is a unique individual and their racial, linguistic, religious and cultural backgrounds should be respected.

- Parents and children should be actively involved in their health care.

- Services should be accessible and child friendly.

- Children have rights that should be respected and promoted.

- Services should be evaluated regularly to ensure that they are meeting the evolving needs of the population.

- Services should be co-ordinated at one moment in time and have continuity over a period of time.

- Agencies should share common objectives and work together within the resources available.

5.2 Local assessment of needs

The practice of community child health rests upon a thorough knowledge of paediatrics combined with an in-depth understanding of the locality in which it is practised including the population, environment and services. The delivery of care should be sensitive to these local needs. The medical, nursing and therapy time allocated to individual schools will be expected to vary widely according to the nature and needs of the population. Other local needs, such as interpreters, should also be considered. The school nurse and paediatrician can play an important role in the assessment of health needs within a school. Formal responsibility for assessment of the health needs of the population and allocation of resources is part of public health medicine. Profiles of individual school populations are an essential tool for this exercise.

5.3 Consent

The issue of consent in relation to community child health services has been considered by the BMA community health doctors' subcommittee. Problems arise where there is no written consent and whether the absence of a response can be interpreted as implied consent. On other occasions we may be uncertain whether the invitation actually reached the home, or the child gives a verbal assurance of parental consent. If parental consent is refused, what information can be given to the school in the interests of the child? Are general consents to a service sufficient to cover the whole range of procedures that might apply? These and many other examples of grey or difficult areas are highlighted by the BMA committee. Most districts will have local guidelines with a specific signed consent at school entry to opt into a school health programme and individual consents for procedures such as medical examination or immunisation. Most would assume that initial consent remains valid unless specifically withdrawn. Obtaining consent may require forms in different languages, the use of interpreters or signing systems of communication. The presence of parents is clearly the best safeguard, but there still remain many circumstances where this is not possible. Parental consent needs to be viewed together with the right of young people of sufficient understanding to give or withold their own consent to examination, (Children Act 1989). Purchasers may wish to see the local policy on consent.

5.4 Confidentiality

Issues of confidentiality relate to records, the wishes of parents and children, and the need of teachers for information. It is good practice to discuss with parents and children the need of teachers to have medical information before discussions with school take place; it is rare for problems to occur if this advice is followed. More difficult areas arise in regard to consent and confidentiality for people under 16. Joint guidance from the BMA, GMSC, HEA, Brook Advisory Centres, FPA and RCGP in 1993 state that *"any competent young person, regardless of age, can independently seek medical advice and give valid consent to medical treatment"* and *"the duty of confidentiality owed to a person under 16 is as great as that owed to any other person"*. This advice is clearly of great importance with regard to contraception. The guidance given to teachers in the 1993 Education Act does not give young people the protection of confidentiality.

5.5 Role of parents as carers

The Children Act 1989 endorsed the responsibility of parents for the care of their children. Unless issues of individual confidentiality arise with regard to a young person, doctors and nurses working with children of school age should ensure a proper two way flow and discussion of information with parents.

5.6 A child centered service

One of the guiding principles of the Children Act 1989 is that the welfare of the child is paramount. This important principle should be applied to the health services for children at school.

5.7 Collaboration

Child health services require a high level of interdisciplinary co-ordination, both within the health services themselves and with other important agencies such as education and social services. The success of community paediatric services rests upon this successful co-operation and communication. Major problems in the past, for example in child protection, have often been related to breakdown or imbalance in this network. The workload that is generated by "networking" is substantial. It requires not only time and will, but also knowledge about the professional disciplines of the other agencies.

The important interfaces of the service within health care are with primary health care teams, hospital paediatric departments and other hospital specialists, (for example ENT, ophthalmology, orthopaedics, genetics), community paediatric nurses, child and adolescent psychiatry, public health, health promotion units and adult secondary care services. Sharing of information contained in *personal child health records* and hospital letters is of immense value. It should be standard practice to obtain parental consent to disclose or discuss clinical information with a third party.

Sharing written information alone is not sufficient. Regular face to face contact is required, for example with colleagues in general practice. Training needs to include knowledge about the work of related disciplines. Ideally this should include some direct experience. Close local co-operation should lead to the development of local agreement and protocols on issues such as referral pathways and clinical management.

Collaboration is not only required at a service level, but also at a planning level, for example joint service plans with education and social services as highlighted in the Audit Commission report *Seen, but not Heard.*

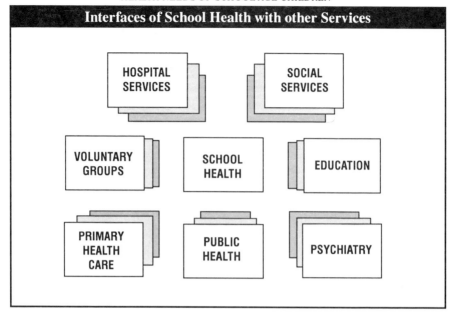

Interfaces of School Health with other Services

HOSPITAL SERVICES

SOCIAL SERVICES

VOLUNTARY GROUPS

SCHOOL HEALTH

EDUCATION

PRIMARY HEALTH CARE

PUBLIC HEALTH

PSYCHIATRY

5.8 Working in schools

The school environment offers a number of unique characteristics and also challenges and opportunities for health gain to which health services for school age children can respond.

- The population is "captive", though we recognise that individuals should give consent.
- The environment is educational.
- The focus is child centred.
- Health and lifestyle are open to influence through curriculum and example.
- Health may be promoted in partnership with teachers and the wider community, (the Health Promoting School).
- The effects of ill health and disability may be minimised in co-operation with teachers.
- Services for *children in need* may be initiated.
- Health monitoring may be offered.
- Ill health, including infectious disease, in the individual and the child population as a whole may be prevented.

The 1981 and 1993 Education Acts have brought more children with special needs into mainstream schools, with increasing demands for specialist nursing, therapy and medical care in school. Many mainstream schools, (see section on accommodation), are poorly provided for even in terms of basic medical and nursing care facilities. A balance must be struck between what it is possible to do in an individual school, (where there may be restricted privacy and resources), and what should be provided in a neighbourhood clinic or hospital setting. Whilst a principle should be service delivery within school, this should not mean a lowering of professional standards to an unacceptable level. Some therapy services, for example speech therapy, may often have to be clinic based, either because of there not being sufficient numbers of children in an individual school to warrant a full session, or because of lack of a suitable room.

Activities that can valuably take place within school are individual health interviews and core surveillance programme; self-referrals by pupils to the school nurse; multidisciplinary discussions of pupils with special educational needs; input into school health education programmes,(this included up to 25% of primary schools in a recent study *Health in Primary Schools* carried out by the Institute of Education, London); and individual paediatric consultation where facilities are suitable.

Schools require regular visits by the school nurse and paediatrician to carry out the core surveillance programme and for health care and advice on individual *children in need.* In the study of 100 primary schools quoted above, 41% had a school nurse visit more than three times a term and in 17% visits were weekly. 37% of schools received a doctor visit once a term and 20% received between 2 and 3 visits a term, with 8% having more frequent visits. The frequency of visits will be influenced by the size of the school as well the needs of its catchment population. Regular contact is required in order to build up partnership between parents, teachers and pupils. Continuity is also important. The above study reported that 55% of primary schools had the same nurse over a three year period and 43% the same doctor.

5.8.1 Medication in schools

The reluctance of teachers to take responsibility for giving medicines to children at school and advice from the NUT that they should not do so, has led to great difficulties for children with special needs at mainstream school, where there is no nurse cover throughout the school day. Particular difficulties have arisen with regard to rectal diazepam for children with epilepsy, adrenaline injection for anaphylaxis, and inhalers for asthma.

At present, teachers cannot be required by law to give prescribed medicines, but if they are willing to do so guidance should be available from the school nurse, paediatrician or the child's family doctor. This is outlined in DES Circular 11/90 Staffing for pupils with special educational needs.

The BMA Community Health Doctors Subcommittee have also considered this issue and produced a report, *Medication in Schools,* in 1994. They considered prescribed and non-prescribed medication; regular and emergency administration; and medication requiring assistance from school staff. Different practical issues arise in primary, secondary and special schools and there is also the risk of teachers receiving conflicting advice. This committee highlighted the need for LEAs to formulate local protocols for good communication.

In many cases medication can be prescribed, for example on a twice daily basis, so as to avoid the need to receive medicine at school. For other children, such as those using inhalers for asthma, self-medication is often the answer but schools still need guidance on self-medication.

This working party felt that the growing difficulties around medication in school need to be resolved, but there are complex legal problems involved. A joint working party or conference involving medical, educational and legal opinion is required.

5.8.2 Accommodation and buildings

Buildings used for child health services should be suitable for this purpose, and are governed by health & safety and building regulations. The medical rooms available in schools should provide privacy, be warm and appropriately equipped. Many are bare, drab and uncomfortable, providing an unsuitable environment for confidential medical consultation or examination. (Henshelwood and Polnay, 1994). They may often be prone to interruption by teachers and others, impeding the use of the room for personal and confidential consultation. Sites can include store cupboards, staff rooms, classrooms, offices and converted cloakrooms or toilets. The current regulations for medical facilities in school are basic. Storage of vaccines in the school medical room will depend upon local policy and resources. Space is also needed for therapy, though as already stated, it is often unrealistic to expect to be able to provide this within every school.

5.9 Working in neighbourhoods

A neighbourhood base is required to service a family or families of schools.

This is often in a local health centre, and accommodation for school nurses and paediatricians may be shared with other community based health services. This should incorporate patient waiting and reception areas, accommodation for examination, investigation, treatment and therapy, counselling, research and teaching.

Other facilities required are medical equipment; ramps for the disabled; a play area; toilets and washing facilities; office space and space for record storage; car parking for staff and parents.

Secretarial and clerical support to the school health team should also be accommodated in the neighbourhood base.

The neighbourhood base can be likened to a *specialist corner store*. It is knowledgeable about local conditions and needs, provides easy access to local residents and a specialist consultation service. Joint clinics can also be established where a suitable suite of rooms is available.

5.10 Manpower

This report has already discussed the wide variation in the volume of service required by different families of schools, so that only broad guidelines can be given on levels of staffing. These must be defined locally from assessment of needs. Staffing is required for a core programme delivered to all children and a secondary service for children with special needs. Whilst pupil numbers in total and the proportion of those with special needs will vary from locality to locality, the forces required to deliver the programme will be greater in areas of disadvantage. Problems of poverty, communication, travel and attendance add to the workload. Estimates by the British Association for Community Child Health suggest that a provider unit with 300,000 population will require three consultants, three associate specialists, three staff grade and three senior house officer posts. There would need to be some adjustments to this balance where there are trainees in higher specialist training or academic commitments. These figures comply very well with previous estimates of medical staff needs. The Audit Commission identified very wide variation in medical and nursing staffing. To some extent this reflects population needs and the extent to which secondary services have been developed as the direct involvement of community paediatricians in child health surveillance has decreased. However, there is a *critical mass* of career staff and trainees that is required to support a lively and comprehensive department that has a broad range of professional skills and sufficient mass to support training and audit exercises, liaison with other children's services and a realistic rota for on call duties in the community.

Recommendations for school nurses have ranged from 1:1500 to 1:2500 school children. However, workload is again more important than caseload as health needs can vary very widely from school to school. We recommend that staffing should be based upon the health needs of individual school populations rather than pupil numbers.

To be successful, this staffing model needs support from therapy, secretarial, clerical and information services. The latter are essential if professional nursing and paediatric time is to be used most effectively. A legacy of poor levels of secretarial support greatly reduces the impact of this service and, as pointed out by the Audit Commission, the lack of data collection and management systems do not allow easy identification of ineffective or poorly delivered services.

5.11 Information

This report and many others have already drawn attention to the need for good data collection. This service, with its roots in public health and its organisation based upon localities must be able to collect individual and population data in order to have an oversight of the health of the school population. Information services must be purchased and safeguarded. Information is required for individual clinical management; for clinical audit; for management purposes in monitoring contracts and individual performance; for recording outcome measures; for epidemiological research; for research and development and service planning. Some guidance on this is to be found in *Community Child Health Services: An Information Base for Purchasers,* (BPA 1992) and *Outcome Measures for Child Health,* (BPA 1992).

Information needs not only to be collected, but also shared between agencies such as hospital services, family health service authorities and the local authority for their registration of *children in need,* required by the 1989 Children Act. Joint commissioning arrangements are recommended in view of the common needs of these services.

Systems should be in place for efficient transfer of information and records when children move from one locality to another. At present, long delays can be experienced and many authorities find themselves in possession of a large volume of records, the subjects of which cannot be traced.

Profile data of a school and its surrounding catchment area are valuable tools for understanding and managing a caseload and to have an oversight of the health of the children in a particular school or locality. The suggested content of a profile is given in the next section. A district *fact file* for each locality would supply a useful base for such profiles and provide some economy to individual nurses and doctors in compiling them. Profile data can be used to compile an annual report for the governors of each school and the director of public health, outlining the health data for the school including cover and outcome of the core programme; health promotion data for the school; special needs statistics; input from the school health team; problem areas, for example accommodation; and recommendations for change in the next school year.

The following issues should be considered when information systems are commissioned:

- Agreed policy on a common data set and the uses that the information will have;
- Accuracy of data collection;
- Literacy in information technology for all staff;
- Knowledge of and access to local and national sources of data;
- Compatible computer systems;
- Meaningful coding of information for school health, (currently being developed);
- Access to users and regular feedback of information;
- Access to epidemiological and statistical advice.

For those of school age the school health module of the national child health system collects the required data set, though different systems are available and operated by some districts. It provides continuity with the pre-school module and collects data on population, surveillance, immunisation and special needs. In Scotland there is a school health module of the national child health surveillance programme, which is attempting to provide a national system for the collection of data.

Health promotion data for individual schools can be obtained from pupil questionnaires such as the Health Related Behaviour Survey Material, produced by the University of Exeter, Schools Health Education Unit, (Balding), or the Trent Lifestyle Survey, (Roberts).

5.12 Recommended data set for locality profiles

Local profiles of schools, families of schools, practice populations or small communities should include information on:

- Environment: location, boundaries, housing, transport, amenities, school buildings.

- Residents: (school and local population), socio-economic profiles, age/ sex structure, unemployment rates, race, ethnic and cultural background, family patterns.

- Health status: Mortality rates, morbidity rates, accident rates, health risks, permanent sickness and disability, hospital admissions, immunisation uptake, uptake of child health surveillance, alcohol and drug dependency, health beliefs, *children in need, (1989* Children Act), known health problems in the school community, known psychological problems in the school community, children with learning difficulties, children on child protection register.

- Service provision: hospital and community paediatric services, (staff, activities, resources, accommodation), general practitioner services, social services, voluntary community activities, education services, family planning services.

These profiles will enable a locally sensitive service to develop and be maintained. Information should be shared with local general practitioners, directors of public health and hospital services and summarised in an annual report to the school governors and director of public health. The overlapping nature of school, practice and community profiles provides a three dimensional model for the study of populations, their needs and service requirements.

Further information on profiles:

National Child Health System
Profiling School Health, HVA School Nurses Subcommittee, 1991
Poverty Profiling, Clare Blackburn, HVA, 1992
School Nursing More than Bumps & Bruises, Brenda Poulton, 1992, Nursing
    Update, Vol7, 2
School Profiling, RCN, 1992
Standards of Care School Nursing, RCN, 1991

Further information on Pupil Questionnaires:

John Balding, Schools Health Education Unit, School of Education, University of
    Exeter, Heavitree Road, Exeter, EX1 2LU

Heather Roberts, Department of Public Health Medicine, Queens Medical Centre,
    Nottingham, NG7 2UH

5.13 Models of good practice - description of a locality service delivering effective services

The Court Report, (1976), described the objectives of community child health services as:

- oversight of health and physical growth of *all* children;

- monitoring the developmental progress of *all* children;

- providing advice and support to parents and, where necessary, arranging treatment or referral;

- providing a programme of effective infectious disease prophylaxis;

- participation in health education and training for parenthood.

As services developed and the Court Report was partially implemented, the concept of a community paediatric team with responsibility for services in a locality was developed (Polnay,1984). The roles of these teams were described as:

- prevention, through health education, parent counselling and immunisation;

- child health surveillance leading to early diagnosis and intervention;

- management of children with special needs; child rearing problems; general paediatric problems; and problems related to groups of children within schools;

- advice to teachers, social workers and careers officers;

- evaluation of the health needs of children in the locality and the implementation of new programmes of care where current programmes are inadequate;

- teaching doctors, medical students, community nursing staff.

These earlier models lead on to the programmes of care recommended by this working party to meet the health needs listed below. These programmes will form the next section of this report.

- **Services for all school children**
  - **Health promotion**
  - **Accident prevention**
  - **Core programme for schools**
  - **Infectious disease control and immunisation**
  - **Dental health**

- **Services for children in need**
  - **Disability : developmental problems; behaviour; ill health;**
    critical illness
  - **Social : child protection; children** *looked after;*
    adoption and fostering; disadvantage

The school nurse and paediatrician who are attached to every school, are the core team for these programmes of care, though for individual programmes, this team may need to be much wider and differently focused.

These wider groups may be known as provider consortia. This large number of professions come from different organisations, for example primary health care teams, school nurse and paediatrician, hospital paediatric departments, child and adolescent psychiatry, learning disability teams and have separate management structures. Examples of such consortia are an audiological service for children; an ophthalmology service; a child and family therapy service; a children's orthopaedic service; a child development team; a network for child protection.

In a typical consortium for children with hearing impairment, pre-school surveillance might be performed by the GP and health visitor, the school entry audiogram by the audiometrician or school nurse, the hearing assessment clinic staffed by community paediatricians or audiological physicians, ENT services provided in a hospital unit, hearing aids and speech therapy provided by the health service, the teacher of the hearing impaired from the LEA, and family support from the social work team for the deaf. Purchasers need to be aware of the need to establish these vital inter-agency consortia, and joint purchasing would be most useful in this respect.

Another important example of a **provider consortium** is the district framework for child protection which will involve all health, education and social work staff as well as police and legal advisers. Those elements which form a consortium, (a functional working group), span trusts, DMUs, fundholding practices, education and social services. Their functions overlap and they clearly need to work co-operatively to ensure best outcome and value for money. The converse of this is the unproductive attempts to shift costs from one element of a consortium to another, (the "its not my budget" syndrome).

The total network of professionals needed to provide child health service to the community is very wide and includes doctors, (general practitioners, community paediatricians, child psychiatrists, paediatric neurologists, orthopaedic surgeons, ophthalmologists, public health physicians, paediatric audiologists); dentists; community nurses, (school nurses, health visitors, community paediatric nurses, learning disabilities nurses and mental health nurses); health promotion officers; speech therapists; physiotherapists; occupational therapists; orthoptists; audiometricians; clinical psychologists; dieticians; clerical and administrative staff. *"Community paediatricians"* is used here to include all consultant, career grade and training grade doctors working in the community child health services.

The next section goes on to describe in more detail individual service programmes of care to meet the needs listed above.

5.14 Programmes of care

In this third section of the report, we outline our recommendations for the programmes of health care for the school child. These programmes are based upon papers submitted and discussed by members of the working party; invited evidence from professionals or groups as part of the consultation process; and the proceedings of a national school health workshop held in Leeds on 14 May 1993.

As far as has been possible we have presented our information under the headings given below.

Identifying Needs:	Aims and Objectives		
Meeting needs:	People	Places	Collaboration
Content and Process	Technical reports/Research		
Outcome measures	Performance targets		

This format follows the sequence of questions that would be followed in the contracting process. It is consistent with the structure of this report and parallels much in the **1992 BPA Report,** *Community Child Health Services: Guidelines for Purchasers.* Technical reports refer to detailed studies of the subject based on a full literature review. The recognition that we are unable to be fully comprehensive in following this framework identifies the areas where more research is required.

Services for All Children

6.1 Health Promotion

Health promotion includes: teacher led sessions in the classroom; one to one advice by the school nurse in health interviews; as well as community activity, for example on sales of cigarettes to children.

Health promotion for the school child is a shared responsibility with schools and their governing bodies, (guided by the Health Education Authority), being responsible for delivering health promotion contained in the national curriculum, and local health authorities for delivering programmes of care to meet *Health of the Nation* targets at all age groups. Much effort needs to go into the development and delivery of health education in schools. In 1993 the Health Education Authority found that in England, only 52% of secondary schools and 41% of primary schools had a health education policy. In only 4% of schools were school nurses involved in writing this policy, but where this did take place their contribution was found to be very useful. Overall the survey found evidence that health education in schools was making progress, though there were concerns about variability in quality, lack of resources for in-service training, and worry that health education may be squeezed by the other demands of the national curriculum.

Health promotion should be an integral part of every consultation between the school nurse and paediatrician, pupil and parents. *(Doctor* derives from the Latin *doceo,* " I teach").

Identifying needs

Many of the *Health of the Nation* targets specifically apply to school children. The importance of this was recognised in titling the conference to celebrate 100 years of nursing in 1992, *The Health of the Nation Begins at School.* Almost all children can be reached through school health education programmes. Children will learn best when they reach their highest attainable state of health and this health gain will continue through adult life. Health promotion should be a priority in services for young people as, especially among adolescents, evidence points to a deterioration in some health indicators such as obesity, smoking, teenage pregnancy. These are reflected in *Health of the Nation* targets.

Important targets related to the school child are: coronary heart disease and stroke, (healthy eating, exercise, smoking and alcohol counselling); cancers, (early recognition, smoking,diet, prevention of skin cancer -doubling of melanoma incidence in the last 10 years and association with severe sunburn before the age of 15); HIV / AIDS and sexual health, (sex education and counselling, family planning advice, advice and counselling on drug misuse); accidents, (prevention, safety measures, education); mental illness, (counselling, personal/social education).

Aims

* To respond to individual requests for information from pupils, teachers and parents;
* To help maintain and develop the school as a healthy environment e.g. hygiene, nutrition, safety, mental health, exercise, communicable disease;
* To work with teachers contributing to their delivery of the national curriculum;
* To work with pupils in planning health education programmes in their school;
* To include appropriate health promotion enquiry and information as part of every consultation.

Objectives

* To decrease the conception rate in under 16s;
* To decrease the incidence of sexually transmitted diseases;
* To decrease the number of children who smoke;
* To decrease the number of children involved in substance misuse;
* To decrease the number of obese school children;
* To promote nutritionally adequate diets;
* To promote increased physical activity;
* To reduce the incidence of suicide, parasuicide and self harm in school children.

Meeting needs

People

The focus of the work of the school nurse is moving towards greater involvement in health promotion as part of the programme of care offered to all children, and as a source of advice to and partnership with teachers as part of the national curriculum. We recognise the shift in emphasis towards health promotion throughout the health service, especially by primary health care teams though they have no specific responsibility for school health in this respect. Parents, peer groups and the media are probably the most important influences. Innovative projects involve children and young people in the design and delivery of specific programmes.

Places
In school classsrooms, in school medical rooms, in neighbourhood clinics and in the wider community.

Collaboration
Alliances are an essential component of health promotion, not just between nurses and teachers, but also in wider whole community based projects. Health promotion officers based in the health services are an essential professional resource.

Content and process
Delivery of health promotion requires that the person involved has correct information on the particular topic, has teaching and communication skills relevant to the age group involved and has teaching programmes and materials of known effectiveness in health promotion. The first two requirements should be met now. Training and updating on health promotion must be a part of every service specification. The third requires much more research and development work to be done to determine which approaches are most effective.

A guide to the topics that could be included for health service input as part of the core programme or as part of school organised group activities are summarised in the table below. This table is not intended to be prescriptive. In an increasing number of schools, the health promotion curriculum has expanded into whole school policies, developing the school as a healthy environment and make it into a "health promoting school". This is part of the European Network of Health Promoting Schools. Programmes should be sufficiently flexible to place more emphasis on areas where there is a locally identified need as well as following national programmes.

	5y	7-8y	11-12y	14y
Adjustment to school	✓	✓	✓	✓
Road safety	✓	✓	✓	✓
Water safety	✓	✓	✓	✓
Diet	✓	✓	✓	✓
Smoking		✓	✓	✓
Exercise	✓	✓	✓	✓
Hygiene	✓	✓	✓	✓
Dental health	✓	✓	✓	✓
Self protection/avoiding abuse	✓	✓	✓	✓
Exposure to sun		✓	✓	✓
Sexual health			✓	✓
Sex education		✓	✓	✓
Drugs		✓	✓	✓
Alcohol		✓	✓	✓
Parenting skills			✓	✓
Teenage counselling			✓	✓
Contraception			✓	✓
Stress & relaxation			✓	✓
Careers advice				✓
Self referrals to school nurse or doctor			✓	✓
Health education as part of national curriculum	✓	✓	✓	✓

Information

Collection and feedback of information, e.g. accidents, dietary information, prevalence of obesity, teenage pregnancy rates and smoking, is in itself not just a monitoring exercise, but can also, through reports to school governors, heighten awareness and exert a positive influence on school policies.

Some issues were frequently highlighted by those who responded to the consultation exercise. These are summarised here, as they represent major causes of concern.

Pregnancy and sexually transmitted diseases
Changes in the national curriculum to exclude teaching on sexually transmitted diseases and restrictions on teachers giving confidential advice on contraception alarmed many doctors and nurses with special interest and knowledge in this field. The importance of advice from the school nurse and paediatrician is highlighted by its absence from educational sources.

School meals requirement for good nutritional standards
Not just a bolt-on to the school, but an integral part of health promotion; recognition that good nutrition is important for good education and that teaching and practice in school should not be contradictory. Although the health services do not carry responsibility for school meals, they should act as powerful advocates for healthy eating in schools and monitors of practice.

Mental health
Promotion of self-esteem and respect for others and continuing and high profile antibullying programmes were frequently mentioned in responses to the consultation report. The role of the school nurse and paediatrician in mental health promotion, (in contrast to the management of problems), warrants greater attention.

Technical reports
Detailed guidance is needed on health promotion on each of the objectives listed above and these should also be related to local circumstances. An example would be the **Health Gain Investment Programme for Older Children and Young People Technical Review** document, produced by the NHS Executive, Trent Regional Health Authority, 1994.

Research
This is a major area for research and development. This should be encouraged at local as well as national level, and promising innovative ideas reported more widely.

Outcome measures
Outcome measures may be distant in time and there are great difficulties in relating changes to any specific intervention. Programmes to teach parenting skills, reduce teenage pregnancy and reduce morbidity in adult life require evaluation ten years or more later with maintenance of the programme over that span of time. Some measures such as teenage pregnancy can be relatively easily obtained. Others related to aspects of lifestyle such as diet, alcohol,

exercise or smoking can be periodically assessed using the self completed questionnaires described in the earlier section on information. Trends in individual schools towards some *Health of the Nation* targets can then be measured.

Performance targets

In our present state of knowledge about what can be achieved, these should be modest. They include proper training for all staff involved in health promotion, a named school nurse with responsibility for liaison with teachers over health promotion in every school, and inclusion in the setting of school health promotion policies.

6.2 Accident prevention

Identifying needs

Accident prevention is a major target area in *Health of the Nation*. Accidents are the largest cause of childhood deaths after the first year of life and a major cause of preventable morbidity and mortality. The major cause is road traffic accidents, accounting for 40% of the total accidental deaths in childhood. Although total deaths from accidents among school children have dropped over the last 40 years, as a proportion of all deaths, accidents have risen.

Accidents account for 120,000 hospital admissions per year in England and Wales and 1.32 million accident and emergency department attendances. 1 in 6 children attend an accident and emergency department every year, resulting in 1 in 5 of all hospital paediatric admissions. The probable yearly cost to the NHS is over £150 million.

Aims

• To reduce the incidence of all accidents among school children.

Objectives

• To reduce the death rate for accidents among children aged under 15 by at least 33% by the year 2005, (*Health of the Nation* target).

Meeting needs

People

School nurses, paediatricians, teachers.

Places
School, home, wider community.

Collaboration
Joint planning involving schools, school nurses and paediatricians, health promotion officers, local authority accident prevention officers, police, planning and transportation departments, public health doctors, accident and emergency departments, is an essential element of the district accident prevention programme.

Content and process
Based on understanding of risks derived from local data collection, developmental level and exposure, journeys to and from school.

Joint planning and policies on a local basis involving schools, school nurses and paediatricians, health promotion officers, local authority accident prevention officers, police, planning and transportation departments, public health doctors, accident and emergency departments.

A multidisciplinary local child accident prevention committee should be established in every district to co-ordinate policy and planning . Paediatricians have a key role to play in these committees. Policies that reduce risks by altering the environment, for example traffic calming schemes, are the most effective.

Local accident data should be reliably collected and distributed to individual school nurses, paediatricians and schools as an essential element in the school profile. Feedback of this data is an important measure to increase awareness and provide an appropriate local focus for teaching programmes in school. Clusters of accidents can be identified in this way and can lead to appropriate environmental changes. Initial collection of accident data will permit the later assessment of the contribution of accidents to disability in childhood.

Safety education is taught as part of school curriculum. Although the major causes of morbidity and mortality take place outside school, environmental change in school e.g. playground safety, classroom safety can contribute towards accident prevention. Schools also provide education on water safety, including swimming instruction. Teaching should include education for pupils, parents and schools on risks and their avoidance. The service should be concerned with risk management as well as risk avoidance, ie learning how to deal with day to day risks. School is a suitable setting to provide this training.

Communities as well as schools can be involved in local accident prevention. Community development and child centred accident prevention programmes such as the Safe Schools Project (Roberts H), can be encouraged.

School nurses and paediatricians can be involved in and promote special schemes to improve access or lower costs of measures such as smoke detectors and cycle helmets.

Clumsy children may be more prone to accidents. Identification of these children by school nurses and doctors and a programme of physiotherapy and occupational therapy could contribute towards accident prevention.

First aid teaching for all should be available through the health services or voluntary agencies.

Local review and follow up of accidents reported through the accident and emergency department, orthopaedic clinics or in-patient discharge summaries can be carried out by the school nurse or paediatrician.

Enforcement of safety legislation and regulation is an essential and effective component of accident prevention.

Research
Research is needed on the relative effectiveness of different types of programme and on targeting of resources for accident prevention. The development of comprehensive district accident databases is needed.

Outcome measures
Reduction of disability secondary to childhood accidents.

Performance targets
To reduce the death rate for accidents among children aged under 15 by at least 33% by the year 2005, (*Health of the Nation* target).

6.3 Core programme for schools

The core programme for schools is the backbone of the programme that we feel should be offered to all children. The health promotion component of this is recorded in an earlier section of this report. The consultation report was widely misquoted, (or misunderstood), as advocating an abandonment of school health checks. It was, instead, confining these to areas where there is clear evidence of benefit, (or reasonably secure evidence) and many districts already operate such a targeted approach. The move towards this will not mean any reduction of time or resources devoted to school health, but will lead to their more effective use. In deciding the content and timing of individual health checks, we have decided not to duplicate the work of other expert groups such as the working parties responsible for *Health for all Children* and the joint working party of the British Paediatric Association and the Royal College of Ophthalmologists, but to include their recommendations within our programme. We have, therefore, not repeated the detailed literature search and discussion undertaken by those groups and we recommend that these publications should be referred to directly.

Identifying needs

9.6% of children under the age of 15 have an illness chronically reducing their functional capacity

10% prevalence rate of psychiatric disorder

5% of school entrants, 8% of 7 year olds and 12% of 11 year olds will have significant visual impairment

5-10% of school entrants will have a significant degree of hearing impairment

47% of five year olds have experienced dental disease

These health problems require medical services for management in their own right, but can also lead to impaired educational progress and special educational needs.

The requirement to provide medical and dental inspection and treatment in all maintained and grant maintained schools is originally stated in section 48 of the 1944 Education Act and currently in paragraph 5 of the NHS Act 1977.

Aims

- To promote the health of children within school;
- To identify children who have problems in health, development, behaviour or who are socially disadvantaged, (*children in need,* 1989 Children Act) and to work with teachers to minimise the effects of these problems upon education.

Objectives

- To ensure the delivery of this key programme to every child of school age;
- To ensure that problems identified through the school health surveillance programme are appropriately referred and managed, (monitoring and recall);
- To ensure that health problems identified through health surveillance programmes are explained and understood by parents and pupils;
- To ensure that health problems likely to have an effect on the pupil's education are explained to the child's teachers.

Meeting needs

People

Every school should have a named school nurse with whom it establishes regular contact. The school nurse should have received specific training for the tasks undertaken in school health surveillance. The school nurse is the key figure in carrying out the core programme, in collaboration with the school paediatrician, and with the help of health care assistants where appropriate. Considerable clerical help is needed to ensure that all children on the population register are reached.

A district child health surveillance co-ordinator working with a senior school nurse has the responsibility to monitor the quality and uptake of the programme and act as a source of advice to purchasers.

Places

In schools. Medical rooms should be properly equipped and essentially provide privacy and relaxing surroundings for health interviews.

Collaboration

Excellent knowledge of and communication with the whole service network for school age children is needed. In particular co-operation with teachers to ensure that partnership is developed and that they are aware of the benefits for education of having a school health surveillance programme.

Content and process

The core programme will be described chronologically, followed by individual sections devoted to measurement of growth, vision and hearing. We realise that some districts or localities may require modifications or additions to this programme based upon the special characteristics or needs of their population. We also recognise that, although there is strong evidence to support some elements of the programme, in other areas more research is required to determine the most effective methods .

It must be emphasised that a core programme provided for all children does not preclude the more detailed assessment of any child at any age where concerns are expressed by the parents, teacher or the pupil him/herself. A high profile, easily accessible service, which communicates its role and availability will be used in this way.

The health checks are linked to opportunities for individual health promotion. The topics for these, appropriate to each age group, are listed in the previous section of the report.

Five years, (school entrant review)

A large volume of research publications focuses on selective and non-selective entrant reviews. These publications are listed in the bibliography.

This will generally take place in the second term of full time schooling when teachers have been able to make an assessment of individual pupils and draw the school nurse's attention to them. In addition to education input, the school nurse will have to draw upon information from the pre-school child health surveillance programme. There will need to be liaison with the health visitor and primary health care team to find out the completeness of the preschool programme and any positive findings emerging from it. Information may be obtained from direct discussion, prepared summaries, original records, and increasingly from parents through the personal child health record.

Although this health check and review at school entry is described as "selective", all children and their parents should be seen. The selective element is in the children who need to be referred to the school doctor for fuller assessment. There is very strong evidence, summarised in the bibliography, that children who have completed an adequate pre-school surveillance programme uneventfully and where school nurse interview, supported by a lack of parent and teachers concerns, indicates that the child is healthy, that there is no additional benefit from the child being seen by the paediatrician attached to the school. This is a very full review. An experienced school nurse will expect to take up to 30 minutes per child.

In this interview, the school nurse is able to introduce herself and explain the service to the parent, obtain written consent for the programme and establish and discuss any parental concerns. Topics for discussion include: completeness of immunisation; completion and outcomes of pre-school surveillance; past medical history; other children in the family, (family tree); current health problems, (particularly diet and growth, vision, hearing, asthma, skin problems, epilepsy, continence) and need for any regular medication at school; concerns about behaviour, (mixing, making friends, anxiety, tempers, sleeping); dental care; family doctor and any other health professionals who are seeing the child.

The elements of examination that form part of this review include, growth, (height and weight), visual acuity and testing hearing. Additional valuable information is obtained from general observation, (demeanour, interaction, confidence, concentration, energy, cleanliness, clothing, dental care).

Results are recorded in the personal child health record, (and any other records that are kept), and relevant positive findings discussed with the parents and, where needed, with the school.

Referral to the paediatrician responsible for the school may be made on the basis of previously identified special needs; new concerns identified at health interview; incomplete information on pre-school surveillance; concerns of parents or teachers. Open discussion between school nurse, doctor, teacher and parents on the need for referral is preferable to a long list of inclusions. Systems of direct referral, for example to a vision clinic or for general health problems to the family doctor, operate in many areas in addition to school doctor referrals.

Seven to eight years, (school year 3)
This is the first year at junior school. Visual acuity and growth monitoring for some children (a) where there is concern about the child's health or growth; (b) when there is incomplete or missing data for the pre-school years, (i.e. less than 3 measurements between 2 and 5 years); and (c) children whose height at 5 is on or below the -2SD line (2nd centile), are the only universal checks recommended at this age. It provides an opportunity for a general health check for children with special needs or where new concerns are voiced; this should, however, be seen as part of the referral or follow up programme.

Eleven to twelve years, (school year 7)
This is the first year at secondary school. A further test of visual acuity is recommended as well as a colour vision test. As at seven, there is an opportunity for a general health check for children with special needs or where new concerns are voiced; this should, however, be seen as part of the referral or follow up programme. New problems may arise at this stage or difficulties revealed by the broader curriculum that is followed.

Fourteen years, (school year 10)
This is the fourth year at secondary school when pupils begin their GCSE courses and where career choice and further education come into consideration. It is also the time of writing the transitional plan for young people with special educational needs. A general health questionnaire is sent to parents and pupils to identify health issues that they wish to discuss. All children are seen by the school nurse for a general health interview. Through these interviews, questionnaires and record information on children with special needs, it is possible to identify those children with health problems, where special careers advice or an appointment to see the school paediatrician is needed. "Ownership" of the management of health problems is moving from parent to child; it is important that the young person is able to identify health problems that he or she is concerned about, be seen by the school nurse or doctor,

obtain information and responsibility for the management of health problems if that is not already the case. This review is an important opportunity for individual health promotion especially related to issues identified on the questionnaire. Important health education topics in this age group include diet, smoking, alcohol, stress, relaxation and sex education.

Growth

Growth monitoring has always been a cornerstone of child health surveillance, with poor growth being recognised as a marker of chronic ill health and social deprivation. Serial measurements of this identified group are a valuable part of the monitoring process for these children, but should not be seen as part of a screening procedure. Similarly, measurement of height and weight may be undertaken because of parental concern, or as part of a health promotion programme to encourage healthy eating and avoid obesity. Teenagers are often concerned about their body image and measurement of height and weight combined with explanation and reassurance may prove useful.

None of the above examples should be confused with the use of height measurement to identify treatable causes of short and tall stature. The recommendations in this report for measurement of younger pre-school children are intended to lead to early diagnosis and, if proved effective under ordinary working conditions, will decrease the contribution that checks at later ages might be making to late diagnosed cases. By the age of five, between a half and three quarters of all children with growth disorders have been identified. Thereafter the number of children remaining to be identified will decrease with successive age bands. Although a case has been made for continuing the routine measurement of children throughout the school years, the ratio of true cases discovered to normal short children becomes progressively less favourable and the cost per case detected rises steeply. The suggestions given in this section can be regarded as reasonable deductions from the current literature, but it must be stressed that their validity has yet to be proved in the field. As in all areas of paediatrics, professional skill and judgement in responding to concerns from parents and children is commendable as complementing formal screening programmes.

Three measurements at 18-24 months, 39-42 months, and at school entry should detect the majority of growth disorders. A fourth measurement at the 7-8 year school nurse check might facilitate detection of Turner's syndrome, late onset growth hormone insufficiency and hypothyroidism. The yield from this may be low, in terms of new treatable disorders, but the costs of measurement would be low if combined with the other elements of the check at this age. Measurement at 7-8 would be recommended for the following groups of children:

(a) where there is concern about the child's health or growth;

(b) when there is incomplete or missing data for the pre-school years, (i.e. less than 3 measurements between 2 and 5 years);

(c) children whose height at 5 is on or below the -2SD line, (2nd centile).

For most children a decision can then be made whether monitoring should be discontinued or undertaken in a growth clinic.

Children should be referred if:

(a) a single height measurement is above the 99.6 or below the 0.4 centile;

(b) the height trajectory crosses a complete channel on the 9 centile growth charts between any pair of measurements;

(c) the child's growth is causing concern to his or her parents.

For districts which continue to undertake height measurement on all children at 7 or 8, this should be in the context of an assessment of the benefits and costs of such a programme. Some districts which have resources for collection of meticulous and continuing growth data for long term audit and research should continue to do so.

Measurement of height and weight should form part of the assessment of all new paediatric referrals, (including eating disorders), presenting to paediatricians or family doctors and in the on-going monitoring of children with chronic illnesses and *children in need*. For children with constitutional delay in growth and puberty, (CDGP), professional awareness of the problem and treatment possibilities should be ensured through health appraisals but no formal monitoring programme is recommended.

Intrinsic to the recommendations for growth measurement is the need for accuracy, correct interpretation and appropriate referral. Training and new equipment may be required to implement the new pre-school measurements. At all age groups a high uptake will need to be achieved. We would make the following recommendations:

• All nurses and doctors working in school should be trained in the technique of measuring height and weight and in the interpretation of growth charts;

• Every school nurse and doctor should have available regularly calibrated and maintained measuring instruments e.g. mini meter and accurate scales;

• Every child's health record should contain an appropriate centile chart on which measurements are plotted, (the 9 centile growth standard charts should be used);

- All children should have their height and weight measured at school entry as part of their overall health assessment, including parental concerns;
- A further measurement is needed at age 7 to 8 for children:
    (a)   where there is concern about the child's health or growth;
    (b)   when there is incomplete or missing data for the pre-school years, (i.e. less than 3 measurements between 2 and 5 years);
    (c)   children whose height at 5 is on or below the -2SD line, (2nd centile).
- Children whose height falls below the 0.4th centile or above the 99.6th centile should be referred without delay to a paediatrician for assessment;
- If a child crosses one complete channel between any two measurements, he/she should be referred;
- Height measurement beyond the age of seven should be continued: if there is chronic disease; for *children in need;* and for a few children where there is doubt about the significance of measurements already obtained, but growth clinic referral is not yet indicated;
- Local protocol must include: referral pathways from the school nurse, community paediatrician and general practitioner; regular audit of the quality of measurement; a regular programme for checking measuring equipment; feedback of information to field staff.

These recommendations for age and referral criteria may require modification in the light of field trials and the yield of treatable conditions in each age group.

Vision

This topic has been reviewed by a working party of the British Paediatric Association and the Royal College of Ophthalmologists.

Vision testing at age five by the school nurse should use a Snellen chart at 6 metres with both eyes being tested together and separately. Vision of 6/12 or worse in either eye should be referred. Children whose visual acuity is 6/9 or whose vision is causing concern will warrant referral if there are other concerns about the child's vision. For children who are unable to cooperate using the Snellen chart, a less developmentally advanced test, such as the Sheridan - Gardiner may be used, or the children referred to an orthoptist in case of continuing difficulty.

This test should be repeated at age 7-8.

At age 11-12 a third measure of visual acuity is carried out, following the same procedure. In addition, a colour vision test should be carried out using the Ishihara plates. Children with impaired colour vision will need a quantitative test such as the City University Plates.

As for all the components of the core programme, correct training must be in place for school nurses and appropriate conditions for testing, (lighting and distance), provided.

Local procedural guidelines must include clear advice to ensure that all children are tested and that those identified are referred, assessed and receive appropriate treatment. The adherence to these guidelines should be monitored.

Hearing

The current sweep test of hearing on school entry at age five should be retained. (Additionally, new pupils into the school should be tested if previous results are unknown, as well as children for whom there is parental or professional concern). The service should also have resources to provide hearing tests for children with special needs who may require a specialist audiology service. The target is to test 98-100% of all five year olds. Approximately 20-25% of children age five may fail a sweep test and this should be repeated 4 - 6 weeks later. Only a small proportion will fail a second test. Procedural guidelines for hearing tests should be available. The criteria for failure are 30 dB at 500Hz and 25dB at 1-4 KHz.

Following screening there should be facilities to proceed to a threshold audiogram and additional tests such as speech discrimination. Districts should have a protocol for management of screening failures with clear referral pathways to the general practitioner, community audiology clinic or ENT clinic.

All staff involved in screening need proper training in audiology and this should be the responsibility of a named person in charge of the community audiology services. The child health services, in collaboration with education authorities, need to provide adequate conditions for hearing testing in schools and annual calibration of audiometers.

"Failures" in the management and outcomes of children in whom a hearing loss has been detected frequently arise from inadequacies in the systems for referral and follow up. Purchasers need to ensure that this consortium operates effectively without such delays. There should be a well defined policy on hearing screening and referral with methods of monitoring the results. Follow up services for children with identified problems must be established. The community audiology clinic should have full diagnostic facilities, and be linked to the child development centre, ENT departments and education and social services.

Summary Chart of recommended core programme

Age	Clinical programme	Immunisation
5 years (year 1)	**School nurse** Structured school entrant health interview conducted with parent Height and weight Check completion of pre-school checks of heart, testes, pre-school concerns Visual acuity Hearing (sweep test) Discussion with teachers to identify any concerns **Paediatrician** Selective referrals from school nurse, taking account of teacher and parental concerns	By age 5 a full course of DT, pertussis, polio, Hib and MMR should have been completed
7-8 years (year 3)	**School nurse** Visual acuity (Height and weight) Opportunity for general health check*	
11-12 years (year 7)	**School nurse** Visual acuity Colour vision Opportunity for general health check*	BCG
14 years (Year 10)	**School nurse** General Health Check Questionnaire to parents and pupils	
14/15 years (year 11)		Dip/T/polio

*More detailed health checks at these ages are required for the individual where there is concern expressed by the child, parents, teacher or from health records; or for the population where school profiles indicate high levels of deprivation or other special circumstances. Height at age 7-8 is indicated (a) where there is concern about the child's health or growth; (b) when there is incomplete or missing data for the pre- school years, (i.e. less than 3 measurements between 2 and 5 years); and (c) children whose height at 5 is on or below the -2SD line, (2nd centile).

Technical reports

A technical report on *Ophthalmic Services for Children* has been published by the British Paediatric Association and the Royal College of Ophthalmologists.

Health for All Children, (3rd edition), will contain a detailed review of screening procedures as an update to the 1992 2nd edition.

Research

Research into skill level required for growth screening, expected yield and cost.

Use of questionnaire to screen for mental health problems. Behaviour problems are the commonest cause of disability in the school age child. The value of other approaches should be explored in addition to referrals and self reported problems as at present.

The key ages chosen are *compromises* between the ages recommended for individual screening tests, educational landmarks such as the transfer to secondary school and the ages at which individual health promotion is likely to be most effective. They are not necessarily the best ages for all of the components. Research to compare the value of alternatively timed appointments is needed. Some have argued in favour of year 6, (the final year in primary school) and year 8, (second year at secondary school), with year 8 giving an earlier opportunity for health promotion work. Selective follow up and careers advice can follow over the next 2 - 3 years. Research is needed comparing the effectiveness of different timings of key health interviews.

Monitoring/Outcome measures

Recording numbers of treatable conditions identified through the core programme, including social deprivation. This should be included in the annual report to the school governors and the director of public health.

A system for review of late diagnosis of health problems in school age children, that could reasonably be detected by the core programme. This could be a responsibility of the district child health surveillance co-ordinator to investigate such cases and make recommendations where necessary for changes in practice.

Performance targets

Uptake measurements of the core programme.

Regular audit of referrals, measuring waiting times, and identifying inappropriate referral pathways.

Surveys of parental, pupil and teacher satisfaction with the service.

6.4 Dental health

Identifying needs
Prevention of common oral disorders - 47% of five year olds have experienced dental disease and approximately 50% of all children have gum disease.

30% of fifteen year olds have active dental decay.

88% of traumatised teeth go untreated.

Only 77% of children age 10-14 are registered with a general dental practitioner.

Aims
- To identify oral disorders and refer for treatment;
- To monitor the provision of dental treatment.

Objectives
- To obtain water fluoridation in all areas, or in its absence provide fluoride supplements for high risk children;
- Increase the proportion of children registered with a general dental practitioner;
- Provide an effective" safety net" service for children who cannot or will not access the general dental services;
- Provide/facilitate access to dental care for children with special dental needs;
- Achieve at least four consultants in paediatric dentistry per region.

Meeting needs
People
Community dental services, general dental services, dental health promotion officers.

Places
Schools, dental clinics, child development centres.

Content and process
- Local and national dental surveys: screening of children's teeth at appropriate intervals, taking into account the local patterns of dental disease;
- Dental epidemiological fieldwork;

- General dental services;
- Targeted service for children with special needs and children in need;
- Dental input to interdisciplinary teams for children with special needs at child development centres and learning disability centres;
- Facilities for dental treatment under sedation and general anaesthesia;
- Dental health promotion for all children in school; provide alternatives to foods and drinks containing non-milk extrinsic sugars as well as fizzy drinks on sale in schools; education programmes for other health professionals on child dental health.

Research
Research projects targeted at specific at-risk groups e.g. teenagers, inner city children.

Outcome measures
Reduction in dental decay in school children.

Special issues
Develop the role of auxiliary care through dental hygienists, oral health therapists and health educators.

Consultation: Jane Goodman, Consultant in Paediatric Dentistry; June Nunn, Senior Lecturer/ Honorary Consultant in Paediatric Dentistry.

6.5 Infectious disease control and immunisation

Identifying needs
Infectious disease is a major cause of illness and absence from school. Significant levels of disability and mortality result as a consequence of some infections e.g. meningitis. Immunisation is a public health programme of undoubted effectiveness for which uptake targets have been set by the Department of Health.

Control of infectious disease in the community is a responsibility of health authorities. Health authorities are required to provide medical advice on control of communicable disease, [HRC (74)19]. In England this is provided by the consultant in communicable disease control, (CCDC). In Scotland, there are consultants in public health with responsibility for communicable disease. Circular [EL(91)123] requires health and local authorities in England to have joint plans for control of communicable disease.

Where there is a threatened epidemic of infectious disease, for example for measles and rubella, the network of school nurses and paediatricians is an effective service for mass immunisation campaigns.

Doctors have a legal responsibility to notify certain infectious diseases. Control of substances hazardous to health regulations 1988 also applies.

Aims

- To reduce the incidence of infectious diseases among school children.

Objectives

- To meet national targets for immunisation uptake;
- To provide a school environment that reduces the risk of spread of infectious disease;
- To limit the spread of infectious disease when outbreaks occur.

Meeting needs
People

Consultants in communicable disease control have overall responsibility for the control of communicable disease in the community.

District immunisation co-ordinators have overall responsibility for the district immunisation programme.

The immunisation of pre-school children is now largely carried out by primary health care teams who have generally reached the high target immunisation levels set. Arrangements for the school age child vary, with some remaining the lead responsibility of the primary health care team and others by the school nurse and paediatrician.

Places

Primary health care teams, schools, clinics.

Collaboration

Close co-operation between schools, school nurses and paediatricians, general practitioners, public health doctors, consultants in infectious disease and environmental health officers is required in the prevention and management of outbreaks of infection.

Content and process

Comprehensive national guidelines on immunisation are set out in *Immunisation against infectious disease,* HMSO, 1992. Districts need to establish practical arrangements for their implementation under the authority of the district immunisation co-ordinator. Districts need to have in place an advisory and training service for immunisation for those who are clinically involved in the programme. A population register and immunisation register should be maintained so that immunisation uptake can be calculated and pockets of unimmunised children identified. Trained school nurses can give immunisations e.g. BCG, and may also immunise those who are not immunised by their general practitioner, according to local prescription protocols.

Education of parents, children and teachers on immunisation and its benefits is a key measure to ensure a high uptake; the school nurse is the lead person in this and in identifying unimmunised children within schools.

Education of parents, children and teachers on the spread of infection and its prevention, (basic hygiene) is also a key responsibility of the school nurse. Districts should have clinical guidelines for school health staff and schools on exclusion of pupils who have infectious diseases.

Districts will require a service to identify and control outbreaks of infectious disease in schools with clear lines of communication and responsibility, (with well known locally agreed procedures); *"intelligence"* on infection within individual schools is an important role of the school nurse. Schools should currently send weekly reports of children with infectious disease to the director of education who then transmits a copy to the school health service. (Responses to the consultation on the draft report indicate that this system is not functional in many districts). A single system of notification to the CCDC would be preferable. The general aim is to control and prevent the spread of communicable disease with minimal disruption to a child's school attendance. In most cases the head teacher would consult with the school doctor, school nurse or CCDC before exclusion.

General arrangements to prevent infectious disease in schools include:

- a service for the proper disposal of clinical waste in schools, education on the management of spillages of blood, vomit and excreta and disposal of sanitary towels;

- appropriate arrangements for food hygiene and general cleanliness in the school e.g. accumulation of litter;

- appropriate toilet and hand washing facilities, (soap and disposable towels), separate from working sinks used for food, washing up or scientific experiments. Younger children will need supervision and older children require encouragement to use them;

- safe clean water supply and sewage disposal;

- proper maintenance of swimming pool and splash pool disinfection and air conditioning plants.

Technical Reports
Immunisation against infectious disease, HMSO, 1992.

Outcome measures
Notification of infectious disease in the community; morbidity and mortality from infectious disease.

Performance targets
Department of Health immunisation uptake targets.

6.6 Adolescent Health

Identifying needs
There is widespread concern about the health of adolescents and evidence of deterioration in some aspects of their health. There are many unmet needs with many districts not making special provisions for this group outside of general paediatrics and adult health. Several of the *Health of the Nation* targets are specifically applied to this age group.

Accidents: Target to reduce death rate from accidents among young people aged 15-24 by at least 25% by the year 2005.

Smoking: Target to reduce prevalence among 11-15 year olds by at least 33% by 1994. Most adult smokers start smoking as teenagers. Older teenagers smoke at nearly the same rates as adults. In the fifth year at secondary school, (year 11), 27% of girls and 26% of boys are smokers.

Drug misuse: Target to reduce the percentage of injecting drug misusers, who report sharing injecting equipment in the previous 4 weeks, by at least 50% by 1997; 5-20% of school age children have "ever tried" a drug; 2-5% use weekly or more often; peak prevalence 14-16 years; age at which adolescents start is getting lower.

Alcohol misuse: About 80% have had "a proper drink" by age 13; only 10% are abstinent by age 17; 30% of boys and 15% of girls aged 13, said they had been "very drunk" in the past year; 5% of convictions for drunkenness were in 14-17 year-olds.

Mental health: Target to reduce the overall suicide rate by at least 15% by the year 2000; suicide in 15-19 year-olds 3 per 100,000; attempted suicides 400 per 100,000.

Conceptions: Target to reduce conceptions among the under 16s by at least 50% by the year 2000; teenage conception rate in England rose from 58.8 to 68.8 per 1000 women age 15-19 between 1980 and 1990; the conception rate for those under 16 showed an increase of 6%; abortion rate in 1991 for those age 14-19 was 18.6 per 1000 women. National survey of sexual attitudes and lifestyles, gave preliminary findings that 30% of people now have sex before the age of 16 and continue to put themselves at risk of HIV.

Mortality: Mortality is low, but improvements over the last 20 years have been less than in any other age group. The commonest causes of death are accidents and malignant disease. In boys age 15-19, suicide and self-inflicted injury are the third most common cause of death.

Morbidity: 1988 OPCS study of disability in Great Britain found disabilities likely to have a significant effect on carrying out everyday activities in 3.5% of 10-15 year olds; nearly two thirds of the children had more than one disability. The figure rises to 20% if milder functional impairments are included, such as uncomplicated asthma, correctable vision or hearing impairments and moderate emotional disturbance.

Disability: Improvements in medical science have led to more young people with disabling conditions surviving into adolescence and adult life. Conditions such as cystic fibrosis, haemophilia, or chronic renal failure present complex challenges to schooling and career development, but also teenagers with these disorders must deal with the burden that chronic ill health adds to the normal adolescent struggle for self-esteem and independence.

Emotional and behavioural problems: Rise in prevalence in teenagers and conditions such as anorexia nervosa and schizophrenia become manifest in this age group. There is evidence that some conditions, including anorexia and depression, are becoming more common.

Aims
• To promote the health of young people.

Objectives
• To develop programmes of care to achieve *Health of the Nation* targets for this age group.

Meeting needs
People
Specialist nurse and doctor in each district with expertise in adolescent problems and needs. Named school health team for every school with access to and communication with teachers and young people. All of these people require up to date information on teenage culture.

Places
Schools, clinics, teenage clinics, hospitals.

Collaboration
Regular liaison and information exchange is needed between school nurse, paediatrician and school. Regular liaison is also required with primary health care teams, accepting the sensitivities surrounding requests for confidentiality. There is also the need to work closely with health promotion departments, child and adolescent psychiatry and local social service departments.

Content and process
Characteristics
The services required for adolescents have several special characteristics if they are to be effective and used: family planning and sexual health services for young people must be "customised" to their access and needs; confidentiality must be assured; services need a high profile, should be well publicised and accessible in timing and place for young people; they should be non-judgmental.

The approach should be to enable them to make choices about their health and to develop self esteem, (low self esteem and a fatalistic approach to their future are recognised as important issues in teenage pregnancy and also very common among children *looked after.*)

The service should consult with young people and involve them in service planning.

The service should include young people who are absent from school for authorised or unauthorised reasons as well as those who are attending.

The services for adolescents include the following elements
General health monitoring and immunisation as a continuation of child health surveillance programme that covers all children and young people.

Information for young people covering health promotion, health and occupation. This is provided through regular sessions in school with drop in sessions e.g. during lunch hour. There should be an active contribution to policy and planning within the school, (personal/social education, parenting skills).

The service should be available to advise teachers and careers officers.

The period of adolescence may extend into the mid-twenties for those with learning disabilities. Paediatricians should be sensitive to the changing needs of young people with learning disabilities and the health promotion and emotional needs that young people with disabilities have in common with all other teenagers. For young people with statements of special needs under the 1993 Education Act, the medical contribution towards the transitional plan looking ahead to school leaving is a major and important activity.

A service to meet the health needs that are special to adolescents: the management of organic illness needing hospital care in an environment suited to their emotional and social needs; care of emotionally disturbed adolescents; genetic counselling; appropriate transfer of care to adult services.

A central drop in clinic outside of the school setting is able to provide information and counselling, easy availability of contraceptive supplies and advice, emergency contraception, pregnancy testing and has the access characteristics that are acceptable to this age group.

Technical reports
Reports giving examples of good practice in adolescent health services. The development of services for adolescents in the UK is very much behind those established in other countries where specialisation in adolescent health is much more common.

Research
Our services for this age group need to be built upon sound research based upon the key areas identified by *Health of the Nation* targets - this includes a better understanding of the factors influencing the adoption of healthy or unhealthy lifestyles; the development of reliable information systems to record key area data; examination of the effectiveness of different service programmes.

Outcome measures
In the short term a reduction in teenage conception rates; however, the desired longterm results of improvements in adolescent health are improvements in physical and mental health in adult life.

Performance targets
Individual *Health of the Nation* targets for this age group. Appointment of a senior nurse and doctor with responsibility for adolescent health. Establishment of a training and updating programme for all staff who work with adolescents; record numbers of staff who have received this training.

Special issue
Homelessness among adolescents is increasing. Special programmes should be developed to meet the health care needs of this highly disadvantaged group of young people.

Services for Children in Need

This section of report describes the programmes of care for those children who would be described as "in need" under the 1989 Children Act.

Children are defined by the Act as being **in need** if:

(a) They are unlikely to achieve or maintain, or to have the opportunity of achieving or maintaining, a *reasonable* standard of health or development without the provision of services by the local authority

(b) their health or development is likely to be significantly impaired, or further impaired, without the provision

(c) they are disabled

7.1 Children in need: Disability

This section covers those children in need who have a defined medical or behavioural problem. They fall within this definition of the 1989 Children Act and may also require assessment under the 1993 Education Act leading to a statement of special educational needs. The health authority has statutory duties under both acts.

7.1.1 Developmental problems

This programme includes the specialist services for assessment and management of children with disabilities including physical and learning disabilities, hearing, vision, speech and language problems. This is a multidisciplinary process covering the work of child development centres, community based services in special and mainstream schools and community clinics. The health authority is required to provide advice to the local education authority and to contribute towards statements and reviews under the 1993 Education Act. The term *educational medicine* is often used to describe the

---

paediatric contribution towards our understanding of children with special educational needs. *Educational medicine,* as an area of paediatrics, is one of the major specialist skills practised by community paediatricians.

This report cannot go into details of assessment or management of any of the vast range of clinical conditions which may be managed by a child development centre. This is the task of a textbook.

Identifying needs

Required under the 1993 Education Act and 1989 Children Act to enable every school child to achieve full potential.

360,000 children with disabilities in the UK, (3% of child population).

147,310 children in England & Wales with statements under the 1981 Education Act.

1.3% of children in mainstream schools have a statement of special educational needs.

Cerebral palsy has increased steeply among very low birth weight babies affecting, on average, 9% of these children.

Aims

- To provide an appropriate and properly resourced health service for the care of the child and family in order to ensure that children reach their maximum potential;
- To provide a service that is comprehensive, co-ordinated and continuous *(seamless);*
- To work in partnership with parents;
- To work in partnership with the local education and social services.

Ojectives

- Early identification of children with special educational needs through child health surveillance;
- Easy access to parents and children where needs arise;
- To provide with other agencies comprehensive, multidisciplinary and continuing assessment and management of the child's needs;
- To provide advice to the local education authority within the time limits set in the 1993 Education Act;
- To provide clinical continuity until the child is referred on to adult services;
- Regular planning, review and monitoring of services for individual children.

Meeting needs

People

School nurses, community paediatric nurses, paediatric physiotherapists, occupational therapists, speech therapists, community paediatricians, consultants in developmental paediatrics and childhood handicap, paediatric neurologists, ophthalmologists, audiologists, orthopaedic surgeons, child and adolescent psychiatrists, clinical geneticists, clinical psychologists, specialist dental services, social workers, teachers, secretarial and clerical staff. A designated doctor carries responsibility of co-ordinating advice to the local education authority and acts as a central point for communication. The core team at the child development centre is usually the paediatrician and therapy staff for day to day management, though there is wide variation in which staff are based at the centre and the range of other disciplines who attend on a sessional basis. Children will have a *named* person from each of the disciplines that are seeing them.

Places

Child development centre, community clinics, special and mainstream schools, in the home.

Collaboration

Inter-disciplinary working is an essential feature of this service with close local networking of health, education and social services. This pattern of work is also reflected in the provisions of the 1989 Children Act and the 1993 Education Act. Cooperation will also occur through the moderating groups to be set up under the 1993 Education Act to determine a local consensus on individual issues. The register of disability required by the 1989 Children Act requires close cooperation between health services and the local authority; school nurses and paediatricians will need to discuss registration with parents and advise on the process.

Content and process

The service can be looked at in two parts: the specialist child development centre and the locality based services within school and local community, (school nurse and paediatrician). The relationship between the two is variable and should be *seamless,* examples being *outreach* from the CDC into the school; *inreach* from the community based service into the CDC and indeed many staff may be common to both environments. Children with special needs at school will need the same services as are provided for all children, for example health education and immunisation, and general medical services from their family doctor, as well as the extra elements of assessment and therapy. In some districts the child development centre will manage all developmental problems; in others there will be subspecialty teams, for example for severe learning difficulties, physical disability, hearing assessment, visual impairment and speech and language problems.

Information

A district special needs register from which information can be extracted for individual management, joint service planning, epidemiological investigations and clinical audit. An information resource centre for parents, children and professionals.

Identification and referral

Children with the most severe developmental problems should be picked up early in life or through attendance at special follow up clinics, as they are known to be at high risk because of factors identified at birth. Other children will be identified through parental concerns about developmental progress in the first years of life and will be known to the health visitor and general practitioner through the pre-school child health surveillance programme. Timely transfer of this information from general practitioner based child health surveillance to community paediatric services is needed to avoid undue delay in paediatric assessment and in assessment of special educational needs. A third group will have learning difficulties that are not apparent until they start school; for these children paediatric referral will be from school.

Assessment

A child development team to provide comprehensive multidisciplinary assessment of children with special needs. For children below school age this will usually take place in the child development centre, but for older children and those with less complex problems, the focus will move from the CDC to the school and local community clinic. This *seamless* service should combine the concentration of resources and expertise within a child development centre with the flexibility to deliver services in other locations, especially school. The response to the consultation report strongly indicated the wide variety of service structures in place for assessment. The main determinants of this variation seems to be history, geography and philanthropy. The essential requirements are that children's needs are met; that specialist skills are available; that support and advice are available to parents and teachers; and that specialist staff can work together as a professional team. Special schools will usually have their own therapy staff, but for the growing numbers of children in mainstream schools, resources and manpower may only be provided efficiently in the child development centre.

The findings, and recommendations following assessment should be widely disseminated to all those who have responsibility for the child, including parents, the family doctor and the CDC and community staff. In addition, paediatric advice is given to the education authority, (1993 Education Act) as an essential part of assessment of special educational needs. This will include the initial statement, annual reviews and contribution towards the transitional plan. At this point consideration needs to be taken of transfer of care to the adult or young adult specialist services, as well as future involvement of social services under the Disabled Persons Act 1986. A summary for the family and the general practitioner is useful at this stage with a detailed and coordinated plan for services after leaving school.

Management
Following assessment, there is a process of regular planning, review and monitoring of services for and progress of individual children. This will take place at school and may be complemented by review in other places such as the child development centre or the hearing assessment centre. Therapy and support, (medical, nursing, physiotherapy, occupational therapy, speech therapy, clinical psychology, social work,) on a day-to-day basis will generally be at school for children attending special schools. Liaison between home and school with the primary health care teams and with teachers is a continuing part of the management process. The personal child health record can provide a good vehicle for communication between the various agencies. Continuity of care is a great advantage for children with complex and severe problems and is highly valued by parents and children.

Resources
Equipment and accommodation for physiotherapy, occupational therapy and speech therapy. Provision of aids and appliances.

Support
Advice, support and counselling to parents and children is an important element of the service. Support for parent groups and voluntary organisations can offer advantages over professional support. Respite can be offered from health, social services or voluntary groups.

Education
Training, updating and support of professional staff.

Special issues

- *Equity of access to service provision*

  Some groups of children pose particular problems with regard to access to the comprehensive range of services that may be required by children with special needs. Travelling families are particularly vulnerable, (see later section on disadvantaged children), and the children of some armed forces families may have problems in continuity of care because of greater mobility. The families of children from ethnic minorities may also have difficulties in using the existing services; employment of interpreters and link workers will aid this process. Independent day and boarding schools may not be able to access the same range of services as maintained schools; for boarders who are some distance from home, communication between health and education services can be poor or non-existent. The special needs of children *looked after* by the local authority will be discussed in a later section of the report; they have a high prevalence of developmental problems, are likely to be identified late through poor or non -attendance at child health clinics and also to be managed poorly through non-attendance and non-compliance. Whilst *looked after* they often continue to have sub-optimal management of their special needs in spite of the 1989 Children Act requirement for a health care plan.

- *Resource allocation*

  Advice on individual children may be determined by needs, but also restricted or confined by resource implications. The ability to be prescriptive in recommendations and to set clear goals to be achieved through that provision might enable us to be more precise in quantifying for purchasers what is required.

- *Increase in mainstream provision*

  Resource and organisational difficulties for school health have arisen with the move towards more mainstream placements for children with special needs. Whilst the advantages of this for the children are clear, if properly resourced, the difficulty of stretching specialist paediatric, nursing and therapy services over an increased number of sites must be acknowledged. The economic and staffing implications of this trend require further analysis.

Technical reports

A series of technical reports giving benchmarks for assessment and management would be of immense value to purchasers and providers.

Research

Staffing, resources and progress of children in mainstream and special school. Districts vary greatly in the way they deliver this service, particularly assessment.

Outcome measures

General outcome measures are difficult to specify because of the vast range of conditions included within special needs and the large range of severity within conditions. The most important outcomes are long term in adult life and are very difficult to relate to specific interventions.

Performance targets

Timeliness of referral, assessment and advice to the local education authority.

7.1.2 Emotional and behavioural problems

Identifying needs

Emotional and behavioural problems sufficiently severe to be disabling were found in 2.1% of all children (aged up to 16) in Great Britain in 1988. This survey by OPCS revealed behaviour problems to be the commonest cause of disability in childhood.

One year prevalence rate for child psychiatric disorder in the general population is around 10%, but much goes unrecognised; 20% of primary and secondary school age children have emotional and behaviour problems; prevalence of depression 2-5% in adolescence; prevalence of delinquency 3% of 10-11 year olds.

The *Health of the Nation* specifically identifies mental health as one of its key areas and has introduced targets to reduce ill health and death due to mental illness, (suicide); the suicide rate is 3 per 100,000 for the age group 15-19 years.

3,000 children are permanently excluded from school because of emotional or behavioural difficulties. These children must not be excluded from the programmes of care described in this report.

8,000 children in residential school because of emotional or behavioural difficulties. These children are also vulnerable to falling through the net of health service care.

Greater risk of child psychiatric disorder in families suffering socio-economic disadvantage or family discord; following child abuse; in association with physical illness; in association with learning difficulties, (40% of children with IQ below 50); in young offenders, (one third of those sentenced aged between 16-18).

Needs may be assessed from national research statistics such as those given above or from locally collected data such as: deaths from suicide, special needs registers, child protection registers, children *looked after* by the local authority, children receiving special education for learning disability and emotional disturbance, homeless families, children in bed and breakfast accommodation, unemployment rates, police and probation statistics, truancy rates. These data should be interpreted with care.

The rate of child psychiatric disorder is much the same as that in adult life. Children form approximately 20% of the total population, but it is rare for more than 5% of the mental health budget to be allocated to children.

In a national review of services for the mental health of children and young people, (Kurtz 1994), 15% of districts had fewer than one child and adolescent psychiatrist; three quarters of EBD schools reported inadequate support; one third of child and adolescent psychiatry teams had lost some social work input in the last three years and educational psychologists had been largely withdrawn from multidisciplinary clinics. The report estimated that paediatricians probably treat more emotional and behavioural disorder than any other professional group.

Aims
- To reduce ill health and death, (suicide) due to mental illness.

Objectives
- To identify children from the school age population who have emotional and behavioural difficulties;
- To provide a programme of management to help these children and their families;
- To establish a programme of mental health promotion.

Meeting needs
People
Many different professional groups are involved in services for children with emotional and behavioural difficulties: primary health care teams; school nurse and community paediatrician; clinical and educational psychologists; local education services; social services; child and adolescent psychiatrists. They vary in their roles in mental health promotion and in the severity of difficulties that they are able to manage with a continuum of provision from straightforward advice on parenting from primary health care, through more difficult problems that might be managed by a community paediatrician, to

the most complex and severe that require the service of child and adolescent psychiatrists. With this continuum of care there are advantages for child psychiatry being included as part of a combined child health service.

Places

Primary health care, schools, neighbourhood clinics, child and adolescent psychiatry centres.

Collaboration

Close co-operation between all services in the planning and provision of all services that have a role in the identification and management of emotional and behavioural problems: these include child and adolescent psychiatry services, school health services provided by the school nurse and paediatrician, local education services, social services, primary health care teams, clinical and educational psychologists, hospital paediatric services. Co-operation also needs to take place in the development of strategies for primary prevention; this should be targeted on vulnerable groups and involve co-operation with social service departments.

Content and process

Planning

In view of the wide range of agencies that have responsibility for children with emotional and behavioural difficulties or on whom these difficulties impact, discussion needs to take place on joint commissioning and planning of services by purchasers with education and social services, as all three agencies have major roles and dilemmas. In particular, there is the need to define carefully the services for management of emotional and behavioural problems among children with learning difficulties; currently this often falls through the nets of community paediatrics, child psychiatry, education and social services because of lack of coherent joint policies. Other important groups are children excluded from school, children *looked after* by the local authority, children in residential special schools because of emotional and behavioural difficulties and children who are the victims of child abuse; services need to planned for all these groups.

Primary prevention and mental health promotion

This may involve preparation for parenthood as a part of school health promotion programmes and training and support of parents through child health clinics and family centres. School policies to combat bullying and promote self-esteem among pupils should be seen as important aspects of mental health promotion. Primary prevention can also be targeted on groups known to be vulnerable, such as families suffering socio-economic disadvantage or family discord. Social services may have an important joint role in this work.

Early identification
Through school nurse health appraisal, parental, teacher or GP referral. We need to recognise the clinical overlap with developmental delay, hearing and language problems, social disadvantage, learning difficulties, abuse and neglect.

Early intervention

? CAMHS

Early intervention, and rapid and appropriate response (secondary prevention), to avoid later exclusions.

Services
The service should be user friendly, high quality, effective and flexible. It also needs to have a high profile and easy access to parents and teachers. Users of the service should be free from stigma. Services should be greatly increased in view of the level of unmet need.

Comprehensive and *seamless* service with ease of referral and opportunities for discussion between paediatricians, school nurses, clinical psychologists, educational psychologists, child and family therapy teams, social service teams. The service is able to provide a range of programmes ranging from simple advice and support, through to more intensive out-patient, day-patient and in-patient service provided by the child and family therapy team.

The child psychiatry service should be provided by a multidisciplinary team which should include a consultant child and adolescent psychiatrist, (one per 100,000 population), psychologists, appropriately trained nurses, therapists, social workers and teachers, the precise composition of the team depending upon local needs and functions.

Comprehensive assessment including evaluation of developmental, health, (e.g. hearing, speech, nutrition, epilepsy), social, family and environmental factors and constructive advice to parents and teachers. Assessment and treatment should be available in a variety of settings as well as the child mental health service base.

Training
Training in management of emotional and behavioural problems is essential for all school nurses and doctors. Training in child psychiatry is particularly important for community paediatricians. Continuing education, advice and supervision should be available for all groups.

Technical reports

Mental health services for children in residential schools, *looked after* by the local authority, excluded from school or following abuse or neglect.

Research

Need for research on prevention of emotional and behavioural problems and targeting of programmes, (identify precursors, predictive factors). Need for research on early identification.

Outcome measures

These may be distant in time with the most important ones being in adult life. There are also many other influences other than the service provided. For the population, the use of mental health screening questionnaires could be explored. Data on substance misuse, exclusion from school, nonattendance at school, children beyond parental control and juvenile offending may be useful measures.

Performance targets

There should be recognition that help for children with emotional and behavioural problems is time intensive and that only counting of contacts is not helpful. *Health of the Nation* targets for mental health to reduce by 33% the suicide rate for all ages.

7.2 Ill health

The term "health needs of school age children" rather than "school health services" has been used throughout this report to emphasise that although *educational medicine* is a central component, other related areas in social paediatrics and general paediatrics are also prominent. "Community paediatrics" includes all the specialist paediatric services that are delivered to a community within that locality.

A locally based paediatric referral service can be responsive to local needs and closely linked to local general practitioners, schools and social service departments. The service can provide communication, teaching and support to primary health care teams. Referral clinics can be established within individual general practices. Joint clinics can also be set up between consultant and other community paediatricians, school nurses, trainees, or therapy staff to provide a substantial and comprehensive service. Joint clinics can also be developed with child and family therapy, and other medical and surgical specialists. These may be based in schools as well as in clinics or GP premises, provided there is suitable clinical accommodation. The service delivered is in most ways similar to the hospital children's out-patient clinic, but families have easier access to clinics that are based in their locality.

Identifying needs

3 % of the general child population is seen in a general out-patient clinic every year. The majority of these, although requiring the opinion of a paediatrician, do not require the use of clinical resources that are not readily available in the community.

Aims

- To establish community referral clinics for general paediatrics;
- To reduce unnecessary hospital referrals for general paediatrics.

Meeting needs

People

Community paediatrician, school nurse, health care assistant.

Places

Neighbourhood clinics, GP premises and schools.

Collaboration

Primary health care teams and specialist community paediatric services. In a combined child health service clinics can be organised to have the most efficient combination of hospital and community clinics.

Content and process

The content and process are the same as for any other type of clinic:
appointment system;
reception staff;
facilities for history taking and examination;
access to laboratory and other investigations;
access to other services, (e.g. dietetics, clinical psychology);
treatment facilities;
secretarial services.

A district standard for these clinics should be set in relation to each of the above headings.

Research
Relative costs of hospital and community clinics. This will in some cases include the costs of upgrading the status, accommodation and equipment of some community clinics. In some cities such clinics have been established for many years, creating opportunities for comparative studies with districts that centralise their general paediatrics.

Performance targets
Waiting lists;
Waiting times;
Attendance rates;
Patient and referrer satisfaction.

7.3 Critical illness

Identifying needs
Approximately 20,000 children are likely to die in the UK from a life-limiting or a life-threatening illness before reaching adulthood.

Aims
- To combine expert medical care with continuing support at home and school.

Meeting needs

People
Hospital and community paediatricians, community paediatric nurses, school nurses, primary health care team.

Places
Home, school, children's hospice, hospital.

Collaboration
Between hospital and community paediatric services, primary health care teams, home and school.

Content and process
The essential elements of this service are:

- expert medical care and counselling from those familiar with the particular condition; liaison with the primary health care team;

- support, information and involvement of the child and family in decision making; symptom relief;
- financial support, (benefits);
- home paediatric nursing support;
- respite care, (children's hospice or in own home);
- support for continuing school attendance and work and for education at home, hospital or hospice;
- care in the terminal phase according to the wishes of the family;
- support and counselling of the family after bereavement;
- support and counselling of school friends and teachers after bereavement.

Consultations: *Professor David Baum, Association for Children with Life-threatening Conditions and Their Families.*

8

Children in Need: Social Issues

8.1 Child protection

Identifying needs

Required by the Children Act 1989, Recommendations of *Working Together Under the Children Act 1989*, HMSO 1991.

Real number of abused children unknown, but in 1992, 38,600 children were entered on child protection registers. 59% were aged 5-15 years.

3.7 per 1000 children age 0-18 are on child protection registers: this figure is rising, presumably as a consequence of improved detection.

Up to 85% of reported concern is investigated and up to 30% of referred children are registered. Commissioning authorities should consult with the designated doctor (see below) on the content of contracts for child protection.

Aims

*   To minimise the emotional and physical disabilities which occur as a result of child abuse and to prevent recurrences;
*   To provide a well trained comprehensive service, available at all times, to respond to emergencies and to take part in an integrated plan for prevention, identification, follow up and management.

Objectives

*   All child health staff trained in child protection procedures;
*   Each referred child to be examined within a locally agreed time (guide eight hours), where this is clinically appropriate;
*   Preliminary report to be available within 48 hours;
*   Communication with other professionals as defined in Area Child Protection Committee policy and national guidelines;
*   Attendance of health staff at strategy meetings and case conferences as needed;
*   Follow up as recommended at case conference.

Meeting needs

People

Procedures cover all health service staff.

Designated senior doctor, nurse and midwife to co-ordinate child protection work within their district, (from *Working Together*); overview of service, provision and resources, (including gaps) key role of designated nurse and doctor in contracting. Responsibility within a professional group should be shared to avoid burnout.

Requires clinical manpower, available throughout the day, with sufficient training and experience to prepare individual reports and make recommendations and interpretations for case conferences and courts, (on call rota).

Secretarial and administrative support is required for child protection services. Reports are often needed quickly, necessitating a high level of support.

Places

Appropriate paediatric settings, preferably designed for this purpose, are required for examination to provide privacy and as relaxed an environment as possible.

Collaboration

Inter-agency communication between paediatricians, social services, education, primary health care teams, police, police surgeons, child and family therapy, hospital paediatric services. There is a need to interface with the courts and police on conduct issues.

Content and process

Policy

Policies should be comprehensive including prevention, training, investigation, assessment and management.

Information

Information on district child protection caseload in collaboration with social services, (child protection register).

Prevention

A programme for prevention of all types of abuse through: classroom teaching programmes, and helplines, including parenting programmes developed with the assistance of school nurses and paediatricians; education and support, for parents. This may be specifically targeted at high risk groups.

Identification and referral

All professionals working with children must be able to recognise child abuse and follow procedures for referral produced by the ACPC. They should be trained in these procedures and be regularly updated. Inter-disciplinary training is recommended.

Examination and investigation

Comfortable facilities should be made available for full paediatric assessment including mental health and psychosocial aspects, in an informal child orientated setting.

Initial full paediatric history and examination leading to a written report covering background information, (medical history, disclosure information) and opinion on injuries, development, growth, general health and emotional state. All doctors who are carrying out examinations because of suspected abuse or neglect should have access to advice from the designated paediatrician for child protection.

Joint examinations with police surgeons according to local policy in cases of suspected child sexual abuse.

Participation in case conferences, strategy meetings and provision of reports, (at present less than 10% of case conferences are attended by medical staff).

Child protection work is highly stressful and it is important that there are local arrangements for debriefing, individual and group support.

Therapeutic work

Contribution to child protection plan and long term management of abused children. This includes contributions to risk assessment as well as a child protection plan.

Special issues

Recognition and monitoring of the increasing workload from child protection, (school nurses and community paediatricians), the complexity of many referrals, the time required to follow local protocols and for attendance at child protection case conferences.

Technical reports

Each district should have a standard protocol for examination and reporting. A national standard would be desirable.

Research
Prevention of child abuse and neglect; breaking *cycles of disadvantage*. Future health and development of children on the child protection register.

Outcome measures
The most important outcome measures are mental health in adult life and later parenting skills. However, it is difficult to record these in routine practice as they are so distant in time. Long-term tracking of children on child protection registers may be important.

Performance targets
These may be related to time between request and examination; time to present a written report; attendance at case conference. Standards may be set for clinical audit of examinations and for accommodation and facilities, (including clinical photography and laboratory services). A system for peer review of cases is regarded as good practice. Training and updating of health service staff should be monitored.

8.2 Children *looked after*

This includes children in foster care, in residential children's homes and in secure accommodation. Children in residential schools will also have some common shared needs.

Identifying needs
Required by the 1989 Children Act, medical contribution towards planning and review and placement of children regulations, 1991.

52,000 children *looked after* in England in 1993 of whom 85% are of school age.

Two Thirds of these children age 5-10 are in foster homes, but 86% from 11 years of age are in residential placements.

This group of children is severely disadvantaged in terms of health, mental health, development, employment, school exclusion and poor educational attainment, low self esteem and low expectations, and poor outcomes in adult life.

Aims
* To promote the physical, social and emotional health and development of children *looked after.*

Objectives

- To have an overview of the health needs of children *looked after* and identify gaps in provision;
- To provide advice on child care needs to community home staff, social workers and foster parents.
- To provide individual health care advice to young people who are *looked after.*

Meeting needs

People

Designated paediatric adviser to interpret health reports, advise on health care arrangements and assist in decision making. A link doctor is desirable who is able to make more direct contact with each community home. These appointments require doctors with specialist training and interest.

Places

Schools, foster homes and community homes.

Collaboration

Close local networking of services with schools, social services, primary health care teams, child development team, child and adolescent psychiatry.

Content and process

Information

A common information base with social services is needed (notification of children *looked after).* BAAF forms are available for recording information and assessments. *"My Health Passport"*, (BAAF) can be used by children over eight.

Consent

Consent required for medical examination from person with parental responsibility and from the young person themselves, depending on their understanding.

Assessment

The service should ensure that children *looked after* have received the full child health surveillance programme and additional medical checks as laid down by the 1989 Children Act, including an initial medical examination and written health assessment, leading to a health care plan. The young person needs to be actively involved in the programme of assessment and to feel the *owner* of the health care plan rather than just its subject. The service should be sensitive to issues of race and gender, which may be highly important to the young person, for example choice of a male or female doctor.

Time for individual consultations is often much longer than standard paediatric appointments in view of the complexity of problems, behavioural difficulties, discontinuities of medical care or lack of information, as well as the need to establish trust and rapport.

Individual health needs review and review of family health needs and history, interpretation of reports, assessment, recommendations and follow up may often be extremely time consuming because of the volume and complexity of individual records. This work may be undertaken by the designated medical adviser or the link doctor to the community home.

Many children will require a much more comprehensive assessment of health, mental health and health promotion needs and we recommend that facilities are available to carry out such a comprehensive medical assessment and mental health assessment where needed.

Management

Management may include extra involvement of many groups of staff; school nurses for health promotion, monitoring of health, counselling and support. Paediatricians may need to bring specialist skills in child development and behaviour, learning difficulties, general paediatrics, disability, abuse and neglect, counselling and health promotion; child and adolescent psychiatry will provide time for staff support and individual therapy.

The following tasks, in addition to individual health care, are included in this programme: paediatric support and information on medical conditions to staff in community homes; distribution of health information to all relevant health professionals and teachers; and advocacy role on behalf of children.

Continuity of care is vital, as so often children have lost confidence in all types of professional help because of the fleeting involvement of individuals. For each young person, continuity of care from one person is prized far higher than a *service* that does not guarantee or offer this.

Training and support

Inter-agency training and discussion are required to promote the understanding of health issues among residential social workers and others responsible for this group of young people.

Technical reports
Health needs assessment guidelines for children *looked after,* setting quality standards.

Research
Need for research on the health needs of children *looked after* and the best ways of meeting those needs.

The adverse outcomes in adult life are a major issue; follow up studies are needed to see how these can be improved.

Outcome measures
Comparison of *Health of the Nation* targets for children *looked after* with the general population.

Performance targets
Audit of medical assessments on children *looked after* against quality standards.

8.3 Adoption and fostering

Identifying needs
Adoption Agencies Regulations, 1983.

Requirement to assess health and development needs.

In 1991, 7,171 adoption orders were made in England & Wales of which 59% involved children aged 5 years or over.

Many of these children have previously been *looked after* and share the complexity of health, developmental and behavioural problems found in this group.

Aim
• To provide informed and timely medical advice to adoption panels.

Meeting needs
People
Medical adviser to adoption agency with specialist paediatric knowledge. Other doctors carrying out examinations for fostering and adoption also require specialist training in emotional, behavioural and developmental problems.

Collaboration
As in all aspects of paediatrics covered in this report, the work is inter-disciplinary involving access to and sharing of records.

Content and process
Medical adviser to adoption agency is responsible for collection, collation, interpretation and distribution of information on health and development to the adoption panel. The adviser must have protected time and adequate administrative support to cover the clinical, advisory and liaison functions. Initial training and continuing medical education is required for doctors involved in this work.

Age appropriate BAAF forms should be used for health and developmental information.

Special issues
Inter-country adoption involves inter cultural or transracial placement of a child. There is often a lack of past information on health and development. Some are concerned about the effects of removing children from their own society and culture.

Outcome measures
Past research on the outcomes of children in cohort studies, showed the superior performance in some areas for children who are adopted compared to the general population. The children placed for adoption have changed since that time with many fewer babies and more older children and those with disabilities. It is still important to monitor the short and long term outcomes, though special studies may need to be set up to do this.

8.4 Disadvantage

School health services were first established at the turn of the century in response to the recognition that disadvantage in childhood leads to poor health in adult life. Current research, such as that of Barker, continues to identify that link. As well as health, educational attainments are adversely affected. Health services for school age children are at this unique crossroads between health, education, social services and the political climate in which wealth is created and distributed. We, therefore, cannot avoid the conclusion that a programme of care for these children is not a *cure* for poverty but a medical response to *diminish* the effects of poverty on health. We should recognise the social and financial contribution towards inequality in health. We, as a group, should point out in all of our assessments of health need, how these are affected by disadvantage and the extent to which inequalities in health exist. We can target our own resources on this group of children and families and advocate that others do the same. This is what is meant by a caring society.

We can point out the health costs (and education, social work and employment costs) of social disadvantage and the effectiveness, especially in the long-term of early intervention programmes. This was recognised as long ago as 1904 in the *Report of the Interdepartmental Committee on Physical Deterioration.* The services that are developed require strong inter-agency collaboration and continuity over time. The body of this report starts and finishes with disadvantage and the 1904 report; perhaps that is what community paediatrics is about?

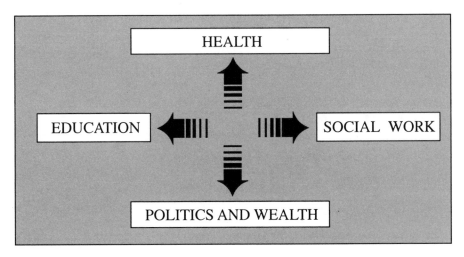

Identifying needs
Required under 1989 Children Act to identify *children in need.*

Social disadvantage makes a major contribution towards educational, developmental, health and emotional problems. Resources targeted on social disadvantage will contribute towards prevention in those areas.

Will have important implications for *Health of the Nation* targets eg. diet and smoking where there are greater problems among disadvantaged groups.

This group includes children aged 5 to 16 years, (or older if still in school):
who are living in temporary accommodation;
belong to traveller families;
are not registered with a general practitioner;
whose parents are unemployed;
whose parents are in unskilled manual occupations;
children of lone parents;

whose families are in receipt of social security benefit, (family credit, income support);

whose parents suffer from chronic illness, the young people often taking the role as carers to the detriment of their own health and education;

whose parents are imprisoned;

who are *looked after* by the local authority; children in residential care.

People living in bed and breakfast accommodation are high users of in-patient beds, Accident and Emergency departments and paediatric clinics.

Ethnic minorities tend to live in poor housing with poor amenities and to have high rates of unemployment. Perinatal mortality is higher and some conditions are more common e.g. tuberculosis, sickle cell anaemia.

• Local data should be collected on:
  - homeless families;
  - traveller families;
  - families in poor housing;
  - unemployment;
  - poor families receiving income support, family credit, free school meals;
  - lone parents;
  - ethnic minorities;
  - families with overwhelming difficulties;
  - children who are caring for an adult with chronic illness, (physical or mental).

Needs will vary widely between and within different health authorities. Collaboration between public health medicine and providers is required for the collection and use of this information.

Aims

• To identify and reach disadvantaged children in order to provide services which aim to achieve optimal promotion of their health and development, prevention of disease, identification of remediable problems, treatment and access to specialist care if necessary. The service should aim to compensate for disadvantage in terms of health and in the longer term, should hope to maximise their achievement in related fields such as education.

Objectives

- Positive discrimination in staffing in deprived areas in terms of numbers of staff, (with relevant training and skills), and continuity.
- Accessible in terms of geography, time, language, (use of interpreters and link workers), culture.

Meeting needs

People

School nurses and paediatricians. The important role and extra workload of primary health care teams in disadvantaged areas is acknowledged.

Places

Schools, communities, locality clinics.

Collaboration

Close local networking and communication with education, social services, primary health care teams, child and family therapy, housing departments, local and voluntary organisations. Particular links need to be established with adult services to identify and provide assistance to young carers.

Content and process

The most effective approaches to meeting health needs are *through special programmes within routine services* e.g. neonatal BCG and screening programmes for haemoglobinopathies; *opportunistic contacts* e.g. at school, clinic, GP surgery, Accident & Emergency departments; *outreach* e.g. to traveller families; targeted work with individual children identified by teacher, school nurse or anyone else; *work with non-statutory organisations* including local youth clubs and community groups.

Continuity of service to a locality is important to build up local knowledge and local trust and recognition. The services should have a high profile and clinics should be welcoming and comfortable. Easy access is important for all age groups. The attitude of staff should be sensitive and non-judgmental, and should respect confidentiality.

Advocacy and service planning and development are as important as direct provision.

Information

Local information is required on a district, locality and individual caseload profile basis. Measures of disadvantage include: free school meals, Townsend index, Jarman index, community profiles, (information on environment and resident population). This information should be linked to routine data collection on immunisation, child health surveillance, hospital attendance, school attendance and special needs. Teachers can contribute both formally and informally to the identification of children living in deprived circumstances.

School profiles must contain criteria for interpretation of *children in need* and this unique information should be made available to social service departments and directors of public health - current criteria are often based upon actual contacts with social service departments and not an overview of the community, (Algate, 1992).

These data can then be used to target resources for prevention, surveillance and management.

Health surveillance and promotion
These programmes should follow on from early intervention programmes with preschool services and nurseries to enhance nutrition, stimulation, child care and emotional well being.

Child health surveillance with special attention to monitoring of growth and uptake of free school meals. More frequent growth monitoring than is recommended in the core programme for all school children is justified in areas where poor food intake is common. The option for full health checks stated in the core programme will apply more often in inner city areas and greater resources needed to deliver the service.

Health promotion is a high priority including smoking, diet, sexual health, exercise, accident prevention, mental health, racism, bullying.

Teaching child care to the next generation.

The service should include advice on state benefits, environmental health.

Secondary care
Comprehensive local secondary care paediatric services are needed in view of the greater morbidity associated with disadvantaged areas. This service should pay special attention to communication with primary care and discuss special arrangements for access on discharge from secondary care. Continuing care demands links to teachers, locality social services teams, voluntary and community groups.

Training
Training to equip professionals with the necessary skills for work in these

complex and demanding areas. Staff support, formal and informal, is also important to ensure continuity of care, protection from overwhelming workload and relief from stress.

Young carers

Children and young people who are taking a caring role frequently go unrecognised. They fear being identified as not coping lest they are removed into care. They suffer physical injuries from lifting, miss out on education and social life, have to deal with the intimate personal care of their parent, whilst being excluded from information and discussion about their parent's medical condition and needs. Dedicated and well advertised support services are needed for young carers to provide advice, information, counselling, respite and help with accessing adult services.

Technical reports

A review, examining in detail the literature and good practice models for community paediatric care in inner city areas, including selective v non-selective approaches to child health surveillance in deprived areas.

Research

Development of deprivation indices specifically for the allocation of school health resources.

Research on development of self-esteem.

Long term research is required on the effectiveness of professional teamwork in disadvantaged areas and their schools.

Children excluded from school and their health needs.

Child health surveillance in deprived areas: what additions are necessary to the core programme?

Outcome measures

The most relevant outcome measure is health in adult life. At present, we have no routine way of obtaining this information other than through special studies.

Performance targets

Clinical audit e.g. immunisation uptake, growth of children in deprived areas. *Health of the Nation* targets, (comparison with other areas).

9

The Way Forward - Agenda for Action

This agenda for action brings together the main themes that have emerged.

A school health report

The need for good information at a locality level has emerged as a key requirement for purchaser and provider alike. It should be a priority to collect this profile data for each school or family of schools. Data are only of value if they are interpreted and used. We recommend, therefore, that these data form the backbone of an annual report to the school governors and the director of public health to give information on the health of the school population, to point out local problems and put forward plans to address unmet needs. We consider this local responsibility, to have an oversight of health as well as to deliver a programme of care, is an essential feature of this service. This would facilitate alliances between school governors, school nurses and paediatricians. A *district factfile* of information containing, for example, population data should be assembled and made available to school nurses and paediatricians to form a basis for locality profiles.

Programme provision- all children

An effective and efficient surveillance programme

We recommend a core programme for child health surveillance for all schools, whether maintained or independent, based on a school nurse interview with parents and children at school entry, with selective medical examination of children with problems, together with school nurse health reviews at 7, 11 and 14 years. The elements of this programme are outlined in the body of this report. This programme, with selective referrals of school entrants to the paediatrician, will permit more effective targeting of resources but will not lead to a reduction in nursing or paediatric staffing. The school nurse has the key role in delivery of this programme and in communicating with schools. We recommend that the accommodation used in school must provide privacy and a suitable environment for health interviews and examination. Specific signed consent for the school health programme should be obtained at school entry and remain valid until school leaving, unless withdrawn. The service delivered in schools should have a high profile and be easily accessed by pupils, parents and teachers.

Infectious disease remains an important cause of ill health and absence from school. The maintenance of a high uptake for immunisation and awareness of hygiene measures to prevent the spread of infection remain priorities for this service.

The importance attached to the *Health of the Nation* targets for school age children should be matched by a growing commitment of the service to health promotion. This should include active involvement in multidisciplinary accident prevention groups, individual health promotion as an essential part of consultations, and wider involvement as adviser or active participant in school health education programmes. Those who undertake this work must possess the necessary teaching skills and health information. More research and development is required in innovative health promotion programmes and those in place should be subject to evaluation in the short and long term.

Adolescent health features prominently in *Health of the Nation* targets, with evidence of deterioration in some measures such as smoking and teenage conceptions. We recommend that each district appoints a specialist nurse and paediatrician with expertise in adolescent health problems to overview the services for young people and put forward plans for a customised service to meet their outstanding health needs.

Evidence that dental health of some parts of the population is deteriorating, highlights the need for continuing programmes for prevention, including health promotion and water fluoridation, and for all school children to be registered with a general dental practitioner.

Effective targeting of services for *children in need*

There is a duty for health authorities to provide services for these children under the 1989 Children Act and the 1993 Education Act.

Children with developmental problems require a specialist and multidisciplinary service for assessment and management. Priority should be placed on early identification and referral. The child development centre and locality based services in schools and clinics should together provide a *seamless* service. Those working in *educational medicine* should receive specialty training in disability and work closely with parents, schools and social services.

Evidence cited in this report, identified emotional and behavioural difficulties as the major cause of disability in children of school age, yet in many districts there were large areas of unmet needs. Since behaviour problems impact so sharply upon education and social services as well as health services, we recommend joint planning. Each district should have a programme for mental health promotion in addition to the service for referral of identified problems. Paediatricians and school nurses have a major role to play in this service, complementary to that provided by child and adolescent psychiatry. We recommend that training in the management of emotional and behavioural problems is essential for both paediatricians and school nurses.

The management of general paediatric referrals in the community is a growing part of the health service for school age children, with the advantages of local access, knowledge and communication. We recommend that such clinics, if not already in place, should be established.

Each district should establish a policy and resources for continuing support of children with critical illness both at home and at school.

Child protection follows national and local guidelines with a designated senior nurse and doctor carrying lead responsibility. District programmes should include prevention as well as identification and referral, investigation and follow up.

Children *looked after* as a group are severely disadvantaged and have poor health, mental health and educational attainments in adult life. A designated medical adviser is recommended to overview the health needs of these children and the type of health assessment that is made to inform their individual health care plans. This person carries responsibility for providing health training and support to residential social workers as well as ensuring that health, mental health and health promotion needs are met.

Adoption and fostering require a designated medical adviser with specialist knowledge in this area.

Childhood disadvantage and the practice of *social paediatrics* remain important tasks for the services to meet the health needs of school age children. Disadvantaged groups, who are *children in need,* need to be identified through health services to schools and programmes of care specifically targeted. The extra resources required to meet the greater workloads of disadvantaged areas needs to be recognised when these are allocated. These targeted services should include all the programmes of care, but especially the core programme, health promotion and secondary care.

Named doctors and nurses

Every school requires a named nurse and paediatrician with special training in *educational medicine* and the health of children and young people. Suggested caseloads and population figures are given in the body of the report, though wide variation is expected in allocation within districts in view of the varying needs of localities. However, a *critical masss* needs to be reached to provide the wide range of skills required, to establish healthy professional teamwork and discussion and to prevent professional isolation. *Named doctors and nurses* will have responsibility for communication with the local education authority;

child protection; for children *looked after;* for adoption and fostering; as district child health surveillance coordinator; district immunisation co-ordinator; leadership of the child development team and for overview of services for adolescents.

Training a priority

Advances in the quality and changes in breadth of the service rest upon the establishment of specialist training for school nurses and community paediatricians and the maintenance of a programme for continuing education for both of these groups. We recommend that very high priority be given to training and continuing education and that this should be included within contracts. The number of trainees should also be sufficient to maintain the workforce at its present level. We recommend that academic training in community paediatrics should be established in every medical school. Training should include a strong interdisciplinary element to facilitate understanding and collaboration, examples being opportunities for community paediatricians to train in general practice and child psychiatry and to learn about the important roles of key therapy staff, (physiotherapy, occupational therapy, speech and language therapy), in the management of children with disabilities.

Interdisciplinary collaboration is essential

Collaborative working is a cornerstone of the health services for children of school age. Contracts should include the requirement and the time for interdisciplinary and interagency communication. In particular, we recommend the development of *district consortia* for particular programmes of care, strong local networks with education and social services and agreed local protocols for referral and management with general practitioners.

Professional management

We recommend that management arrangements for health services for school age children should provide identified professional as well as service leadership.

Technical reports

Benchmarks for assessment and management for children with developmental problems.

Mental health problems in children in residential schools, children *looked after,* children excluded from school, or following abuse or neglect.

Investigation of child abuse and neglect.

Health needs assessment of children *looked after.*
Models of good practice for inner city areas.

Research requirements

The academic base of the subject needs to be expanded and many areas reviewed in this report require further research. We recommend that the following should be the subjects of specific research proposals.

Research and development is needed on the effectiveness of programmes for health promotion.

The relative effectiveness of different types of programmes for accident prevention and on the targeting of resources.

Child development teams function very differently from district to district. Comparative studies of different service models would be useful.

With greater numbers of children with special needs in mainstream schools and a declining special school population, some analysis is needed of the resulting changes in staffing, resources, organisation of services and the benefit for children.

The use of questionnaires in identifying mental health problems in school age children, in contrast to the present arrangements through referral and self reported problems.

Factors that influence the adoption of healthy and unhealthy lifestyles among adolescents.

Reliability of information systems to record key data on adolescent health.
The effectiveness of different models of service provision for adolescents.
Prevention of emotional and behavioural problems, early identification.
Prevention of child abuse and neglect.
Effective programmes of care for children *looked after.*
Development of self-esteem.
Health needs of children excluded from school.

Special issues
Medication in schools
There is an urgent need for clear and authoritative guidelines on giving medication to children at school. We recommend that an expert medical, nursing, education and legal group is established to provide these.

Independent schools
We recommend all school children should receive the same programmes of care, including those who attend independent schools. We recommend that a working group is established with the Medical Officers of Schools Association

and representatives of the Independent Schools Joint Council to make recommendations on how this may be achieved.

Appendix

Bibliography

Legislation and governmental publications

Assessing Health Care Needs. *A DHA project discussion paper; National Health Service Management Executive* 1991;

Bridges over troubled waters. *NHS Health Advisory Service on Services for Disturbed Adolescents. HMSO ISBN 1851970533*

Children Act. *HMSO London ISBN 0105441899* 1989;

Children Act, Guidance and Regulations, Volume 5 Independent Schools, Volume 6, Children with Disabilities. 1989;

Children Act 1989 - an Introductory Guide for the NHS. *London, HMSO* 1991;

Convention on the rights of the child. *United Nations, Treaty Series 44, London HMSO ISBN 0101197624* 1992;

DHSS, Prevention in the child health services. *London, DHSS* 1980;

DHSS, Health and social services statistics for England. *HMSO, London* 1987;

Education (Scotland) Act 1980 (and subsequent amendments)

Education Act 1981. An Act to make provision with respect to children with special educational needs. *London, HMSO* 1981;

Education Act 1993, Code of Practice, *DFE*, 1994

Education Act 1993, Pupils with Problems, *DFE*, 1994

Education Act 1993, Development of Special Schools, Circular 3/94, *DFE*, 1994

Education Act 1993: Sex Education, Circular 5/94, *DFE*, 1994

Education Act 1993, The Organisation of Special Educational Provision, Circular 6/94, *DFE*, 1994

Education (school premises) regulations 1981, part 3 para 12.

Education Observed. *11, Hospital and Home Education Services, DES* 1989;

A guide to arrangements for interagency co-operation for the protection of children from abuse. *Working Together, HMSO*, London: ISBN 1113214723 1991;

Fit for the Future. Report of the Committee on Child Health Services (Court Report). *London, HMSO, Cmnd 6684* 1976;

Getting in on the Act: provision for pupils with special educational needs London, *HMSO*, 1992

The Health of the Nation, Key Area Handbooks. *HMSO* 1992;

Health of the Nation - a strategy for health in England. *Department of Health, HMSO, London*, 1992

Inequalities in Health. *Report of a Research Working Group (The Black Report)* London, DHSS 1980;

Investing in the future. Child health ten years after the Court report. A report of the Policy and Practice Review Group. *National Children's Bureau. London* 1987;

NCH, Children in Britain 1992: The NCH Factfile. *Factfile: Publ. NCH, 85 Highbury Park, London N5 1 UD ISBN 090098421X* 1992;

OPCS, Social Survey Division General Household Survey 1987. *HMSO, London* 1989;

Neighbourhood Nursing - A focus for care. *Report of the Community Nursing Review (The Cumberlege Report). London,* DHSS 1986;

Protocol for Investment in Health Gain, Maternal Early Child Health. *Welsh Health Planning Forum* 1991;

Recommendations of the Working Group on Indicators for the Community Health Services. *DH* 1990;

Scottish Health: A Challege to Us All, *Scottish Office Home and Health Department, HMSO,* 1992

Seen but not heard, *Audit Commission,* 1994

Special educational needs. *Report of the Committee of Enquiry into the Education of Handicapped Children and Young People (Warnock Report)* 1978;

Special educational needs: Implementation of the Education Act 1981. *Third Report from the Education, Science and Arts Committee, Session 1986-87* 1987;

Staffing for pupils with special educational needs, *DES Circular 11/90*

Strategic Intent and Direction of the NHS in Wales. *Welsh National Planning Forum* 1989;

Towards better health care for school children in Scotland. *A report by the Child Health Programme Planning Group of the Scottish Health Service Planning Council, Edinburgh, HMSO* 1980;

Warnock, H.M., Special educational needs: Report of the Committee of Enquiry into the education of handicapped children and young people. *Department* of *Education and Science, HMSO, London* 1978;

National & Regional Reports and Working Parties

Across the field. *Special Children* 1986; 8-9.

Bridging the Gaps. *Action for Sick Children* 1993;

Bone, M., The prevalence of disability among children. *OPCS surveys of disability in Great Britain Report 3 HMSO, London* 1989;

BPA, Report of the working party on the needs and care of adolescents. *BPA* 1985;

BPA, The school health services: report on the school health services prepared by a committee of the BPA 1987;

BPA, The School Health Service. 1987;

BPA, Health Services for school leavers with a mental handicap. 1990;

BPA, Towards a Combined Child Health Service. *London, BPA* 1991;

BPA, Community Child Health Services. *Guide-lines for Purchasers* 1992;

BPA, Community Child Health Services; an information base for purchasers. *London: BPA 1992;*

Changing School Health Services. *Primary Health Care Group, Kings Fund Centre for Health Services Development* 1988;

Education Act 1981. The law on special education. *Advisory Centre for Education, 18 Victoria Park Square, London E2 9PB*

The flaws in the 1981 Act. *Childright* 1985;

Focus on Community Child Health Services, an aid to contracting, NHS Executive, Trent Regional Health Authority, 1994

Healthier Children - thinking prevention. *Report of a working party appointed by the Council of the Royal College of GPs. London, RCGP* 1983;

Health for all children. A programme for child health surveillance. Hall, D.M.B., *Oxford Medical Publications, Oxford* 1991;

Health promotion in child health Child health surveillance; a time for change Monitoring child health surveillance. *Royal Colleges of Physicians of the UK, Committee on Health Promotion* 1989;

ILEA, Educational opportunities for all? The report of the committee reviewing provision to meet special educational needs (The Fish Report). *London, ILEA* 1985;

Kurtz, Z., The challenge to health services for children of school age in inner London, ILEA 1990;

NACRO, Preventing Youth Crime: National Association for the care and resettlement of offenders. *169 Clapham Road, London SW9 OPU* 1991;

Nursing and Child Protection, RCN, 1994

Outcome Measures for Child Health, BPA, 1992 Profiling School Health. *HVA School Nurses Subcommittee* 1991;

Project Health. *HVA* 1991;

Roche, K. and M. Stacey, Overview of research on the provision and utilisation of child health services in the community. *Department of Sociology, University of Warwick, Coventry ISBN 0947829105* 1991;

The School Health Service, Faculty of Community Health of the Society of Public Health. 1991;

School Nursing More than Bumps & Bruises, Brenda Poulton, 1992, Nursing Update, Vol7, 2

School Profiling, RCN, 1992

Sexually Transmitted Diseases. UK *Levels of Health. First Report, Faculty of Public Health Medicine of the Royal College of physicians, London* 1991; June:45-52.

Targets for Health for All. *World Health Organisation Health for All 2000, Regional Office for Europe, Copenhagen* 1985;

Working Together for Tomorrow's Children. *BPA/FPHM* 1990;

Changing contexts

The family

De'Ath, E., Focus on families: Divorce and its effects on children: Briefing paper. *Children's Society, Edward Rudolf House, Margery St London WClXOJL* 1988;

Elliot, B.J. and M.P.M. Richards, Effects of parental divorce on children. *Arch Dis Childhood* 1991; 66:915-916.

Lambert L, Streather J, 1980, Children in changing families, Macmillan, London

Wicks M, 1989, Family Trends, insecurities and social policy, Children & Society, 3; 67-80

The Health Service

Bowie, C. and A.P. Jones, Court come true - for better or for worse? *Br Med* J 1985; 298:1322-1324.

Øvretveit, J., Co-ordinating Community Care. *Open University Press, Buckingham* 1993;

Polnay, L., H. Bingham, and R. Tamhne, Contracting for child health services in the community. *Arch Dis Child* 1993; 68:517-521.

Polnay L. 'The Community Paediatric Team - an approach to child health services in a deprived inner-city area', In: *Progress in Child Health, Vol 1*, Ed. A Macfarlane, Churchill Livingstone, 1984

Shepherd, S., Aspects of the Children Act - a medical perspective. *Health Trends* 1991; 23:2:51-53.

Child Health

Birch, J.M., *et al.*, Improvements in survival from childhood cancer: results of a population based survey over 30 years. *Br Med J* 1988; 296:1372-76.

Forfar, F., Child Health in a changing society. *Oxford University Press ISBN 0192616870* 1989;

Kurtz, Z., Investing in the future - what is happening to children's health in the UK? *Children and Society* 1988; 4:335-341.

Woodroffe C, Glickman M, Barker M, Power C, Children. Teenagers and Health, the Key Data,

Open University Press, 1993

Woodruffe C, Glickman M, Trends in Child Health, Children & Society, 1993; 7; 4963

Wyke, S. and J. Hewison, Child Health Matters. *Milton Keynes Open University Press* 1991;

Consent and confidentiality

Age of Legal Capacity (Scotland) Act 1991

BMA Central Committee for Public Health Medicine and Community Health, Consent in Community Child Health Services, 1994. (Discussion paper)

Confidentiality and People under 16. Guidance issued jointly by the BMA, GMSC, HEA, Brook Advisory Centres, FPA and RCGP, 1993

Manpower

Paediatricians

BPA, Paediatric Medical Staffing for the 1990s, 1990

Davies, L.M. and M.D. Bretman, What do community health doctors do? Survey of their work in the child health service in Nottinghamshire. *Br Med J* 1985; 290:16041606.

Report of the Joint Working Party on Medical Services for Children, NHSME, 1992

School nursing

Anon, A new image for the school nurse. *Editorial, Health at School* 1989; 5:3:

ASNA, Recommended guide-lines for good practice in school nursing. 1992;

Bagnall, P., The way forward for school nursing. *Health Education Journal* 1991; 50:3:

Collins, J., Why educate school nurses? *Health Visitor* 1985; 58:123-124.

Course in School Nursing. *Criteria and Cuide-lines for Practical Experience, ENB* 1991;

Fletcher, K., School nurses do it in schools - trends in school nursing practice. *Amalgamated School Nurses Association, London* 1992;

Hanson, L., No longer the nit lady. *Nursing Times* 1987; 83:22:30-32.

Hawes, M., School nursing in Norwich Health Authority. *Health Visitor* 1989; 62:351352.

Howes, M., School nursing in Norwich Health Authority. *Health Visitor* 1989; 62:351.

Johnstone, J., What do school nurses do? *Health Visitor* 1986; 59:363-364.

Principles into Practice, an HVA position statement on health visiting and school nursing. 1992;

Nelson, M., The changing role of the school nurse within Worcester and District Health Authority. *Health Visitor* 1989; 62:349-50.

Proctor, S.E., Evaluation of nursing practice in schools. *J Sch Health* 1986; 56:272275.

Roger J, School nursing: what teachers think, *Primary Health Care, 1992, 2, 10*

Royal College of Nursing, Recommended guide-lines for the basis role of the school nurse. *RCN Society of Primary Health Care Nursing, London W1* 1981;

Standards of Care. *School Nursing, RCN* 1991;

Survey of School Nursing. *RCN* 1992;

Thurtle Val, School nursing, Moving forward, a process of professionalisation (personal communication,) 1994

Training

Report of the Working Group on Specialist Medical Training, Department of Health, 1993

Report on proposals for the future of community education and practice. *UKCC* 1991; United Kingdom Central Council for Nursing and Midwifery

The future of professional practice

The Council's standards for education and practice following registration March 1994

Information

MacFaul, R., Much data but limited information in the NHS. *Arch Dis Child* 1988; 63:1276-80

Rigby, M., Computing school health information. School care goes hi-tech. *Health and Social Services Journal* 1985; 18 April :486-7

Rigby, M., Child health comes of age. Br J *Healthcare Comput* 1985a; July:1315.

Rigby, M., School care goes hi-tech. *Health Social Service Journal* 1985b; 18:486-487.

Rigby, M.J. The national child health computer system. *Progress in Child Health*. 3. Edinburgh: Churchill Livingstone, 1987: 101-120.

Scrivens, E., Management information in the national health service: the use of the child health computer system. *Community Medicine* 1984; 6:4:299-305.

Winn, E. and C. King, Making use of community health services information. *Kings Fund Centre/report of workshop 3.7.86, Kings Fund Institute, London* 1986;

School Health Services

Bendlow G, Lee J, Mayall B, Oakley A, Storey P, Health in Primary Schools, Social Science Research Unit, Institute of Education, London, 1994

BMA Community Health Doctors Subcommittee, Medication in Schools, 1994 (Discussion paper)

Crouchman, M.R., The role of school medical officer in secondary schools. *Journal of Royal College General Practitioners* 1986; 36:322-324.

Fox, T.K. and *et al*, How schools perceive the school health service. *Public Health* 1991; 105:399-403.

Harrison, A. and J. Gretton. School Health: The Invisible Service. *Health Care UK: An Economic, Social and Policy Audit*. CIPFA, London, 1986: 25-32.

Henshelwood, J. and . Polnay L, Facilities for the school health team, *Archives* of

Disease in Childhood; 1994, 70: 542-543

Jackson, C., School Health: swings and roundabouts. *Health Visitor* 1992; 65:392-393

Loudon, G.M. and J.H. Walker, The school health service and the school doctor: Bridging in health, Oxford: Nuffield Provincial Hospital Trust. 1975;

Macfarlane, A., Child health services in the community: making them work. *Br Med I* 1986; 293:222-223.

Nash, W., M. Thruston, and M.E. Baly, Health at school - caring for the whole child. *Heinemann Medical Books, London* 1985;

Oberklaid, F., It's time - the future of school health in Australia. *Paediatric Child Health* 26:244-251.

Oberklaid, F., Children with school problems - an expanding role for the paediatrician. *Aust Paediatric J* 1984; 20:271-5.

Perkins, E.R., The school health service through parents eyes. *Arch Dis Child* 1989; 64:1088-1091.

Polnay, L. and D. Hull, *Community Paediatrics.* second edition ed. 1993, Churchill Livingstone.

Rutter, M., School Effects on Pupil Progress: Research Findings and Policy Implications. *Child Development* 1983; 54:1:1-29.

The School Health Service, Faculty of Community Health of the Society of Public Health. 1991;

School Health 1991. *Dept Public Health Medicine, Bristol* S *Weston Health Authority* 1991;

School Health Service Review. *South Birmingham Health Authority* 1991;

Survey of school medicals - Society of Public Health. *Faculty of Community Health newsletter* 1992; iv:1:

Turner, R., Healthcare goes back to school. *Health Service Journal* 1986; 992.

Watt, J., A. Faulkner, and S. Farrow, Effectiveness of the School Health Service: Review of the Background Literature. *Health Care Evaluation Unit, Department of Epidemiology and Public Health Medicine: University of Bristol* 1991;

Whitmore, K. and M. Bax, School health in the wilderness. *Health Trends* 1982; 14:3:52-55.

Whitmore, K., M. Bax, and A.M. Jepson, Health services in primary schools: the nurse's role 1. *Nursing Times* 1982a; 78:25:97-100.

Whitmore, K., M. Bax, and A.M. Jepson, Health services in primary schools: the nurse's role 2. Conclusions. *Nursing Times* 1982b; 78:25:103-104.

Whitmore, K. The past, present and future of the health services for children in school. *Progress in child health.* Edinburgh: Churchill Livingstone, 1984: 213-229.

Whitmore, K., Health Services in Schools - a new look. *Spastics International Medical*

Publications, London 1985;

Whyte, E., Health Begins at school. *Nursing Times* 1984; 21:40-42.

Health promotion

Balding, J., Young people in 1988. *Health Education Authority Schools Health Education Unit, Publication, University of Exeter* 1989;

Balding, J., G. Foot, and D. Regis, The assessment of health needs at the community level. *Schools Health Education Unit, Publication, University of Exeter ISBN 0850681162* 1991;

Baric, L., Health Promoting Schools - Evaluation and Audit. l *Inst Health Education* 1991; 29:4:114120.

BMA, Young people and alcohol. *Board* of *Science and Education: BMA Publication* 1986;

Brown T, The Health of the Nation and the National Curriculum, SW Thames RHA, 1994

Cambridge DHA/ILEA TACADE Health Promoting Schools. A training Manual. *TACADE. I Hulme Place, The Crescent, Salford M5 4QA* 1990;

Challener, Health Education in Secondary Schools - Is it working? A study of 1,418 Cambridgeshire pupils. *Public Health* 1990; 104:195-205.

Curtis, H., Teenage Relationships and Sex Education. *Arch Dis Childhood* 1988; 63:935-941.

Gillies, P., *et al.,* An adolescent smoking survey in Trent, and its contribution to health promotion. *Health Education Journal* 1987; 46:1 :19-22.

Goddard, E., Smoking among secondary school children in England in 1988. *HMSO, London* 1988;

Heathcote, G., Teachers, health education, and in-service training. *Health Education Journal* 1989; 48:4:172-175.

The Health of the Nation. *HMSO* 1992;

The Health of the Nation, Key Area Handbooks. *HMSO* 1992;

Health Education Authority Tomorrow's Young Adults: 9 - 15 year-olds look at alcohol, drugs, exercise and smoking, 1992

Health Education Authority, Promoting our Children's Health in Schools: a working partnership, 1990

Health Education in Schools, a survey, Health Education Authority, 1989

Health Education policies in schools, Health Education Authority, 1993

Health Update - Smoking. Health Education Authority, London 1991;

Holliday, K., E. Carter, and E. Cardwell, The school nurse as a health educator. *Health Visitor* 1984; 57:182-183.

National Audit of Drug Misuse in Britain 1992. *I Hatton Place, London EC1 8ND*

NHS Executive, Trent Regional Health Authority, Health Gain Investment Programme for Older Children & Young People, technical review document, 1994

MacFarlane, J A., *et al.,* Teenagers and their health. *Arch Dis Child* 1987; 62:1125-9.

Macfarlane, J A., Health Promotion and children and teenagers. *Br Med J* 1993; 306:81.

NCC, Curriculum guidance in health education. *National Curriculum Council, 15-17 New Street, York ISBN 872676235* 1990;

Nicoll, A. Written material concerning health for parents and children. *Progress for Child Health.* Churchill Livingstone, 1985:

Noble, C., The Health Promoting School and the Market Place. *Education and Health* 1991; 9:5:2-5.

Nutbeam, D., *et al.,* The health-promoting school: organisation and policy development in Welsh secondary schools. *Health Education Journal* 1987; 46:3:109115.

Nutbeam, D., *et al.,* Evaluation of two school smoking education programmes under normal classroom conditions. *Br Med J* 1993; 306:102-107.

Plamping, D., Learning from children learning: peer tutoring in health education. *Radical Community Medicine* 1986; 26:31-40.

Reid, D. and D. Massey, Can school health education be more effective? *Health Education Journal* 1986; 45:1:7-13.

Royal College of Physicians, London, Smoking and the Young. 1992;

Smith, A., The Nations Health - A strategy for the 1990s. *Kings Fund, London* 1988; ISBN 0197246478:

Stone, E.J. and C.L. Perry, An international perspective and comparison of school health programmes. *Journal* of *School Health 1990;* 60:7:291-382.

Tandy, A. and M. Bax, AIDS: health education in schools. The role of the community child health services. *Children and Society* 1987; 2:148-156.

Townsend, J., *et al.,* Adolescent smokers seen in general practice: health, lifestyle, physical measurements, and response to anti-smoking advice. *Br Med J 1991;* 303:947-50.

Whitehead, M., Swimming upstream - trends and prospects in education for health. *King's Fund Institute, London* 1989;

Williams, T., School health education 15 years on. *Health Education Journal* 1986; 45:1:3-6.

Accident prevention

Armstrong A N, Molyneux E. (1992) Glass injuries to children. British Medical Journal 304:360.

Basic Principles of Child Accident Prevention. (1989) Child Accident Prevention Trust, London

CAPT, NHS costs of childhood accidents. *Childhood Prevention Trust, London* 1992; Constantinides P. (1987) The management response to childhood accidents. Primary

Health Care Group.Kings Fund Centre.

Crouchman M. (1990) Children with head injuries. British Medical Journal 301:128990.

Deddenham A, Newman RJ. (1991) Restraint of children in cars. British Medical Journal 303:1283-4.

Drug and Therapeutics Bulletin. (1982) Child Resistant containers now. 20:5.

Levene, S. (1991) Coroners records of accidental deaths. Archives of Disease in Childhood 66: 1239-1241.

Lindrum J, Mason A R, Sunderland R. (1988) Cost to the NHS of Accidents to Children in the West Midlands. British Medical Journal 296:611.

Kemp A, Sibert J. (1992) Drowning and near drowning in children in the United Kingdom: lessons for preparation. British Medical Journal 304:1143-6.

Lowery, S. (1992) Injuries from domestic glazing. British Medical Journal 304:332.

Mayer Hillman, Adams J, Whitelake J. (1990) One false move. A study of children's independent mobility. Policies Study Institute London.

Pless I B. (1991) Accident Prevention. British Medical Journal 303:462-4.

Sharples PM, Stoney A, Aynsley Green A, Eyre JA. (1990) Causes of fatal childhood accidents involving head injury in Northern Region 1979-86. British Medical Journal 301:1193-7.

Sibert J R. (1991) Accidents to children: a doctor's role. Education or environmental change? Archives of Disease in Childhood 66:890-3.

Sibert JR, (1992), Accidents and emergencies in childhood, Royal College of Physicians, London

Towner E, Dowswell T, Jarvis S, (1993), Reducing childhood accidents. The effectiveness of health promotion interventions: a literature review, Health Education Authority;

The core programme for schools

Bhrolchain, C., An audit of the school health service in Litherland over 4 years 198892. unpublished;

Cherry, N., R. Gear, and H. Walden, Occupational health and the school leaver. *Community Medicine* 1983; 5:1 :3-10.

Colver, A.F. and H. Steiner, Health surveillance of preschool children. Br *Med J* 1986; 293:258-260.

Cross, A.W., Health screening in schools. Part II. J Pedintr 1985; 197:5:653-661.

Donovan, C., Practising prevention: children aged 5-15. Br *Med J* 1982; 285:1018

Fitzherbert, K., Communication with teachers in the health surveillance of school children. *Mat Child Health* 1982; 7:3:100-103.

Hodges, M., Screening secondary school children. *Nursing Times* 1983; August:5355.

Holme, C., School medical examinations. *The Practitioner* 1989; 233:1243-1245.

Holt, H., Southampton's health appraisal pilot study. *Nursing Standard* 1990; 4:16:26-27.

HVA, Health Assessment and the School Nurse 1992;

Inglis, J., Health interviews for school children. *Midwife Health Visitor Community Nurse* 1989; 25:5:202-204.

Jones, C. and N. Gordon, The school entry medical examination - what do teachers think? *Child care health and development* 1991; 19:173-185.

Lane, M.G., An evaluation of the 13+ contact in secondary schools in the NW Surrey HA. in press;

Latham, A., Health appraisal/surveillance by school nurses. *Health Visitor* 1981; 51:1:25-27.

Leff, S., A survey of parental concerns as children reach school entry age. *Public Health* 1991; 105:127-132.

Light, L. and J. Elks, Pilot study of health interviews at 13+ years in secondary school. *(unpublished)* 1991

Marks, A. and M. Fisher, Health assessment and screening during adolescence. *Paediatrics* 1987; 80:1, July supplement

Rona, R.J., *et al.*, Referral patterns after school medical examinations. *Arch Dis Child* 1989; 64:829833.

Tuke, J.W., Screening and surveillance of school aged children. *Br Med J 1990;* 300:1180-1182.

Wade, J., E. Sinclair, and J. Bennett, Health care interviews in 20 schools - a review of the first two years experience in the Brighton Health District. *Public Health* 1989; 103:467-474.

Waldron, S., Involving parents in school age checks. *Nursing Standard* 1992; 6:18:37-40

Williamson, T., Health care interviews by school nurses. *Health Visitor 1992;* 65:11:402-404.

School entrants :Selective or non-selective?

Bax, M. and K. Whitmore, The medical examination of children on entry to school the results and use of neurodevelopmental assessment. *Dev Med Child Neurol* 1987; 29:1:40-55.

Bhrolchain, C.N., Routine or selective entrant medical: a review of current literature. unpublished;

Broomfield, R. and J. Tew, Selective medical at school entry. *Public Health* 106:149154.

Houghton and *et al*, Selective medical examinations at school entry; should we do it and if so how? *Journal of Public Health Medicine* 1992; 142:111-116.

James, E.G., Health screening of children entering school in the Rhymney Valley in September 1987: an evaluation of outcome. *PhD thesis, Oxford University* Unpublished;

Kennedy, F.D., Have school entry medicals had their day? *Arch Dis Child* 1988; 63:1261-1263

Leff, S., A comprehensive selective programme of health surveillance at school. *Public Health* 1989; 103:475-484.

Leff S, Bennet J, Improving Decision Making at School Entry Medicals - Completing the Audit Cycle, *Public Health,* 1993, 107, 421-428

Newby, M. and A. Nicoll, Selection of children for school medicals by a pastoral care system in an inner city junior school. *Public Health* 1985; 99:331-337.

O'Callaghan, E.M. and A.F. Colver, Selective medical examination on starting school. *Arch Dis Child* 1987; 62:1041-1043.

Oberklaid, F., The ritual school health examination; an idea whose time has passed. *Australian Paediatric Journal* 1985; 21:155-7.

Oberklaid, F., Selective examinations on starting school. *Arch* Dis *Child* 1988; 63:225.

Resnik, R., D. Starte, and S. Harvey, Health screening at school entry - what is achieved? *Australian Journal of Paediatrics* 1985; 21:159-62.

Richman, S. and M. Miles, Selective medical examinations for school entrants - the way forward. *Arch Dis Child* 1990; 65:1177-1181.

Smith, G.C., *et al.,* The five year school medical - time for change. *Arch* Dis *Child* 1990; 65:225-227

Varley, Y., Health of school entrants in a West Yorkshire Health District in 1989. *Public Health* 1990; 104:473-477.

Voss, L.D., *et al.,* Poor growth in school entrants as in index of organic disease: the Wessex Growth Study. *Br Med J* 1992; 305:1400-02.

Wadsworth, D., Trail of selection of children for school entrant medical. *Leeds (unpublished) 1990;*

Whitmore, K. and M.C. Bax, The school entry medical examination. *Arch* Dis *Child* 1986; 61:807817.

Whitmore, K. and M.C. Bax, Checking the health of school entrants. *Arch Dis Child* 1990; 65:320326.

Zeilhuis, G.A., Are periodic school health examinations worthwhile? *Health Policy* 1985; 5:3:241253.

Growth

Davies, S., Children's growth - how and why schools should measure it. *Health at School* 1985; 1:1:28-29.

Hall DMB ed, *Health for all Children,* OUP, 1992

Macfarlane A, Should we screen for growth problems in children ? Journal of Medical

Screening 1, 50-59

Rona, R.J. and S. Chinn, The national study of health and growth: nutritional surveillance of primary school children from 1972-1981 with special reference to unemployment and social class. *Annals of human biology* 1985; 11:1 :17-28.

Voss L, Walker J, Lunt H, Wilkin T, Betts P, The Wessex Growth Study: First Report, *Acta Paed Scand Suppl;* 1989, 65-72

Vision

Bacon, L., Colour vision defect - an educational handicap. *Medical Officer* 1971; 125:199-209.

Fyfe, J. and D. Ellerbroek, Colour vision defects and the school nurse. *Nursing Times* 1984; June: 48-49.

Fielder AR, Moseley MJ , (1988). Do we need to measure the visual acuity of children? Journal of the Royal Society of Medicine, 81, 380-383

Ingram, R.M., Review of children referred from the school vision screening programme in Kettering during 1976-8. *Br Med J* 1989; 298:935-936.

Shaw, D E, Fielder A R, Minshall C, Rosenthal, 1988, Amblyopia - Factors influencing age of presentation, Lancet, 1988, 207-209

Stewart-Brown, S. Visual defects in school children: screening policy and educational implications. *Progress in Child Health*. 3. Edinburgh: Churchill Livingstone, 1987: 15-37.

Stewart-Brown, S.L. and M. Haslum, Screening of vision in school: could we do better by doing less? *Br Med J* 1988; 297:1111-1113.

Stewart-Brown, S. and *et al*, Educational attainment of 10 year olds with treated and untreated visual defects. *Dev Med Child Neurol* 1985; 27:504-513.

Survey of vision testing - Society of Public Health. *Faculty of Community Health newsletter* 1992; iv:1:

Hearing

Chalmers D, Stewart I, Silva P, Mulveva A, Otitis media with effusion - The Dunedin study, *Clinics in Developmental Medicine* No 108, 1989, Mackeith Press, Oxford, Blackwell Scientific Publications Ltd

Dodds, A.A., Screening for hearing impairment. *Society of Public Health - Faculty of Community Health newsletter iv:11 :*

Haggard M P Hearing screening in children - state of the art(s), *Arch Dis Child.* 1990, 65:1193

Haggard M P and Pullan C R Staffing and structure for paediatric audiology services in hospital and community units, British Journal of Audiology,1989, 23, 99-116

Harding, N. and O. Nietupska, Auditory screening of school children: fact or fallacy? *Br Med J* 1982; 184:717-720.

Hodges, M., Screening secondary school children. *Nursing Times* 1983; August:5355.

Stewart-Brown, S. and M.N. Haslum, Screening for hearing loss in childhood: a study of national practice. *Br Med J* 1987; 294:1386-1388.

Survey of hearing testing - Society of Public Health. *Faculty of Community Health newsletter* 1992; iv:l:

Dental health

Dowell, T.B., The caries experience of five-year-old children in England and Wales. A survey coordinated by the British Association for the Study of Community Dentistry in 1985-86. *Community Dental Health* 1988; 5:185-97.

Infectious disease control & immunisation

Anderson, R.M. and B.T. Grenfell, Quantitative investigations of different vaccination policies for the control of congenital rubella syndrome in the UK. J Hyg 1986; 96:305-33.

Anderson, M., Preventing rubella in Edinburgh and Lothian schools. *Health at School* 1986; 2:2:4041.

Conway, S., BCG Vaccination in children - routine vaccination of school children is not cost effective and could be stopped. *BMJ* 1990; 301:1059-1060.

Cundall, D., Inner city tuberculosis and immunisation policy. *Arch Dis Child* 1988; 68:954-6.

Hall, S., Current epidemiology of childhood infections. *Brit Med Bulletin* 1986; 42:2:119-126.

Immunisation against infectious disease. *Department of Health, HMSO* 1992;

Nicoll A N, Rudd P, Manual on Infections and Immunisations in Childhood, British Paediatric Association, OUP, 1992

Saffin, K., School nurse immunising without a doctor present. *Health Visitor* 1992; 65:394-396.

Shabde N, Waterston T, Screening children from overseas for infections, *British Medical Journal*, 1990, 301, 800 - 802

Adolescent health

Bennet, D., Adolescent health in Australia - An overview of needs and approaches to care. *Health Education and promotion Monograph - Australian Medical Association* 1984;

Bewley, B.R., The inadequacy of adolescent health statistics. *Community Medicine* 1982; 2:97-98.

Chief Medical Officer, Annual Report on the State of the Public Health 1993, The Health of Adolescents, 74-113, HMSO, 1994

Curtis, H., Teenage Relationships and Sex Education. *Arch Dis Child.* 1988; 63:935-941.

Daniels S Teenage Health - a positive alternative for Nottingham Youth. *Teenage Health Care Project, Memorial House, Standard Hill, Nottingham NG1 6FX 1989;*

Dillner, L., Increase in 16 year-olds attending family planning clinics. *Br Med J* 1992; 304:275.

Epstein, R., P. Rice, and P. Wallace, Teenagers health concern - implications for primary health care professionals. *Journal Royal College General Practitioners* 1989; 247-9:

Malus, M., Towards a separate adolescent medicine. *Br Med J 1992;* 305:789.

Rogers J, Disabled adults 16-30; who cares, *Primary Health Care; 4, 8*

Swadi, H., Alcohol abuse in adolescence: an update. *Arch Dis Child* 1993; 68:341-3.

Whiting, K., Towards a school health service for adolescents the teacher-health worker team. *Children and Society* 1990; 4:2:225-233.

WHO, Young people health - a challenge for society. *WHO Technical Report Series: 731, Geneva* 1986;

Woodroffe C, Glickman M, Barker M, Power C, Children. Teenagers and Health, the Key Data, Open University Press, 1993

Developmental problems

Bax MCO, Whitmore K, District Handicap Teams in England 1983-88, Archives of Disease in Childhood, 1991, 66; 656-664

Bone, M., The prevalence of disability among children. *OPCS surveys of disability in Great Britain Report 3 HMSO, London* 1989;

Butler, J., Ensuring access to health care for children with disabilities. *New Engl J Med* 1987; 317:3:162-5.

Evans, P.M., S.J.W. Evans, and E. Alderman, Cerebral palsy - why we must plan for survival. *Arch Dis Child* 1990; 65:12:1329-33.

Lewis, S., Paediatrician to a special school. *Arch Dis Child* 1990; 65:803-806.

Trend, U. and A. Nicoll, Disabled children in a comprehensive school. *Health at School* 1987; 2:4:102-105.

Waldron, S., Integration of handicapped pupils. *Nursing Times* 1983; 54-56.

Yerbury M, The District services for children who are disables - a search for patterns of excellence, M.Phil thesis, (unpublished)

Emotional and behavioural difficulties

Black, D., Mental Health Services for Children. *Br Med J* 1992; 305:971-2.

Calouste Gulbenkian Foundation Bullying - the child's view: 98 *Portland Street, London W1N 4ET*

Cockett, M., D. Kuh, and J. Tripp, The needs of disturbed adolescents. *Children and Society* 1987; 2:93-113.

Earls, F. and K.G. Jung, Temperament and home environment characteristics as casual factors in the early development of childhood psychopathology. *Journal of the American Academy of Child and Adolescent Psychiatry* 1987; 26:491-8.

Garralda, M.E. and D. Bailey, Psychiatric disorders in general paediatric referrals.

Arch Dis Child 1989; 64:1727-33.

Graham, P.J. Behavioural and Intellectual Development. *Childhood Epidemiology.* 42(2). British Medical Bulletin, 1986: 155-62.

Hawton, K., By their own hand. *Br Med I* 1992; 304:1000.

Kurtz, Z., With Quality in Mind, Mental Health Care for Children and Young People. *Action for Sick Children in association with SW Thames, RHA* 1992;

Kurtz Z, Thornes R, Wolkind S, Services for the Mental Health of Children and Young People, a National Review, Maudesley Hospital and SW Thames RHA, 1994

Olweus D, Bullying at School. What we know and what we can do, Blackwell, Oxford, 1993

Richman, N., Behaviour Problems in Preschool Children: Family and Social Factors. *British Journal of Psychiatry* 1977; 131:523-7.

Rutter, M., *et al.,* Attainment and adjustment in two geographical areas. Prevalence of psychiatric disorder. *British Journal of Psychiatry* 1975; 126:563-579.

Rutter, M., Isle of Wight revisited: twenty-five years of child psychiatric epidemiology. *Journal of the American Academy of Child and Adolescent Psychiatry* 1989; 28:633-53.

Tatum, D. and G. Herbert, Bullying - a positive response. *Available from South Glamorgan Institute of Higher Education, Cyncoed Road, Cardiff CF2 6XD*

Troyna, B. and R. Hatcher, Racial harassment in school. *National Children's Bureau 1990;* No 92:

General paediatrics

Anderson, H.R., *et al.,* Morbidity and school absence caused by asthma and wheezing illness. *Arch Dis Child* 1983; 58:777-784.

Bevis, M. and B. Taylor, What do school teachers know about asthma? *Arch Dis Child* 1990; 65:622625.

Effective Health Care - the treatment of persistent glue ear in children. *School of Public Health, Leeds* 1992; No 4:November 1992:

Speight, A.N., D.A. Lee, and E.N. Hey, Underdiagnosis and undertreatment of asthma in childhood. *Br Med J* 1983; 286:1253-1256.

Spencer, N.J., Consultant paediatric outreach clinics - a practical step in integration. *Arch Dis Child* 1993; 68:496-500.

Storr, J., E. Barrell, and W. Lenney, Asthma in primary schools. Br *Med J* 1987; 295:251-252.

Child protection

Report of the committee of inquiry into the care and supervision provided in relation to Maria Colwell. *London, HMSO* 1974;

Baker, A.W. and S.P. Duncan, Child sexual abuse a study of prevalence in Great Britain. *Child Abuse and Neglect* 1985; 9:457-467.

Bebbington, A. and J. Miles, The background of children who enter local authority care. *British Journal of Social Work* 1989; 19: 5

A guide to arrangements for interagency co-operation for the protection of children from abuse. *Working Together, HMSO,* London: ISBN 1113214723 1991;

Children "looked after"

Bamford, F., The physical health of children in care - research needs. *London, Economic and Social Research Council* 1988;

Choosing with care, Report of a Committee on Enquiry, chair Warner N, HMSO, 1992

Garnett, L., Leaving care for independence: a follow-up study to the placement outcome project. *London: HMSO* 1990;

Looking after children. Guide-lines for users of the assessment and action records. *London: HMSO* 1991;

Seen but not heard, Audit Commission, HMSO, 1994

Stein, M., Leaving care and the 1989 Children Act. *Oxford: First Key* 1991;

Utting W, Children in the Public Care, HMSO, 1991

Wolkind, S., The mental health of children in care - research needs. *London: Economic and Social Research Council* 1988;

Adoption and Fostering

Future of Adoption Panels - a consultation document, Department of Health, 1994

International Bar Association. The inter-country adoption process from the UK: the adoptive parents perspective. *London IBA* 1991;

Rowe, J., M. Hundleby, and L. Garnett, Child care now; a survey of placement patterns. *London: BAAF* 1989;

Stone, J., Children in care: the role of short-term fostering. *Report to the City of Newcastle-upon-Tyne Social Services* 1990;

Using the BAAF medical forms. *Practice note 32, London, BAAF* 1994;

Wolkind, S. and A. Kozaruk, The adoption of children with medical handicap. *Adoption and Fostering* 1:32-40.

Disadvantage

Angell, M., Privilege and Health - What is the connection? *NEIM* 1993; 329:2:126-7.

Aldridge J, Becker S, Children Who Care, 1993, Department of Social Studies, Loughborough University

Aldridge J, Becker S, My Child, My Carer, 1994, Department of Social Studies, Loughborough University

Balarajan, B. and B. Botting, Perinatal mortality in England and Wales: variations by mother's country of birth (1982-85). *Health Trends* 1989; 21:79-84.

Barker, D.J.P., *et al.*, Weight in infancy and death for ischaemic heart disease. *Lancet*

1989; ii:577580.

Blackburn, C., Poverty Profiling. *HVA* 1992;

Bradshaw, J., Child poverty and deprivation in the UK. *National Children's Bureau, 8 Wakely St. London ISBN 0902817574* 1990;

Cade, J. and H. Lambert, Evaluation of the effect of the removal of the family income supplement (FIS) free school meal or the food intake of secondary school children. *J Publ Hlth Med* 1991; 13:4:295-306.

Conway, J., Presentation for Poor Health: the Crisis for Homeless Families. *The Maternity Alliance: London* 1988;

Cornwell, J., Improving health care for travellers. *King's Fund, London* 1984;

Feder, G., M.R. Salkind, and Sweeney, Traveller-Gypsies and general practitioners in East London: the role of the Traveller health visitor. *Health Trends* 1989; 21:93-4.

Jefferson, N., G. Sleight, and A. Macfarlane, Immunisation of children by a nurse without a doctor present. *Br Med J* 1987; 294:423-4.

Lowry, S., Health and homelessness. *Br Med J* 1991; 300:32-4.

Lowry, S., Housing and Health. *Br Med J* 1991; 303:838-40.

Oppenheim, C., Poverty: the Facts. *Child Poverty Action Group* 1988;

Polnay, L, Poor Homes and Families, in Polnay L, Hull D, pgs 221-237 Community Paediatrics, Second Edition, Churchill Livingstone, 1993

Rathwell, T., Meeting Needs in Health Planning for Ethnic Minorities. *Medicine in Society* 1981; 7:4:14-15.

Seymore, J., Give us a Chance. Children, Poverty and the Health of the Nation. *A joint statement from the Child Poverty Action Group, the Health Visitors' Association and Save the Children Fund on The Health of the Nation White Paper* 1992; July:

Slater, M., Health for all our children. Achieving appropriate health care for black and minority ethnic children and their families. *Action for Sick Children Quality Review Series* 1993;

Smith, R., Without work all life goes rotten. *Br Med J* 1992; 305:972.

Spencer, N.J., Poverty and child health: an annotation. *Children and Society* 1990; 4:4:352-362.

Turner, S., The Riverside Child Health Project Evaluation Report. *Department of Family and Community Medicine, University of Newcastle Upon Tyne* 1983;

Victor, C.R., *et al.*, Use of hospital services by homeless families in an inner London district. *Br Med J* 1989; 299:725-7.

PERSONS CONSULTED OR WHO SUBMITTED EVIDENCE

Professor David Baum
Dr Martin Bax
Dr Martin Bellman
Dr C Ni Bhrolchain
Dr Hilary Bingham
Dr Mitch Blair
Dr Paul Carter
Dr Hazel Curtis
Dr J M Donnelly
Mr Tam Fry
Miss Janet Goodman
Professor David Hall
Dr Roger Harrington
Dr Ann Howard
Dr Sue Ilett
Dr Hugh Jackson
Dr Cynthia Jones
Dr Elizabeth James
Dr Pat Lambert

Dr Isabel Larcombe
Dr Sonya Leff
Dr Simon Lenton
Dr Sundara Lingam
Dr Aidan Macfarlane
Dr Alison Maddocks
Dr Ian McKinlay
Dr June Nunn
Dr Elizabeth Poskitt
Professor John Pearce
Dr Connie Pullan
Dr Heather Richardson
Ms Phillipa Russell, Council
 for Disabled Children
Dr Paula Sneath
Ms Val Thurtle
Mrs Sheila Waldron
Dr Tony Waterston
Dr Margaret Yerbury

Organisations invited to submit evidence

Health Education Authority
Medical Officers of Schools Association
National Children's Bureau

Persons attending Leeds conference

Dr Paul Gorham - meeting organiser
Dr Liz Adamson
Dr Qutububbin Ahmad
Dr Lilias Alison
Ms Jane Appleby
Dr Chris Bacon
Dr Wendy Billington
Dr Black
Dr Mitch Blair
Dr Peter Bradley
Dr Jay Brock
Dr Leslie Butlin
Dr Paul Carter

Dr K A K Choudhary
Mr Alan Coles
Dr N Cookey
Dr Conn
Dr David Cundall
Dr Dorothy Dalry
Dr Jonathan Dare
Dr Dorothy Hayman
Dr East
Dr Aycliffe Edwards
Dr Margaret Edwards
Ms Dorinda Fitton
Dr L K Hall

Dr Alison Harris
Dr Elizabeth James
Dr Sandra Lane
Dr Sonya Leff
Mrs Mary El-Rayes
Dr Anne Exley
Dr Mike Farrell
Dr DM Hamade
Ms Caroline Hayman
Dr Patricia Henshall
Ms Katherine Hetherington
Dr Ann Howard
Dr Margaret Huyton
Dr Pat Lambert
Dr Francis Lawrenson
Dr J I Mabbott
Ms Rose Marshall
Dr Elaine Martin
Dr Barbara Mary
Dr E A Mason
Dr Joan Maurice-Smith
Dr Marian Miles
Dr Joy Moore

Dr S K Pandey
Dr Karin Parkinson
Dr Leon Polnay
Dr Brian Potter
Dr Isabel Price
Dr Bronwen Robinson
Dr Elizabeth Saunders
Dr Jane Seymour
Dr Jean Shorland
Dr Ron Smith
Dr David Stacey
Dr Georgina Soulby
Dr Francesca Tennant
Dr M Thazin
Dr Amanda Thomas
Miss Ada Thompson
Dr Gill Turner
Dr Caroline Twigg
Dr Z Vermaak
Dr Jan Welbury
Dr Jane Wynne
Dr Margaret Yerbury
Leeds workshop contributers

Persons who submitted comments on the consultation paper

Lee Adams, Director of Health Promotion, *Sheffield Health Promotion Centre*

Christine M B Allen, Joint Chief Officer, *Winchester and Central Hampshire Community Health Council*

Dr C J Allsop, SCMO, for *Shropshire Community Paediatric Doctors' Committee*

Dr A G Antoniou, *Wiinchester and Eastleigh Healthcare NHS Trust*

Dr E Barrie, SCMO, *Frimley Children's Centre, North Downs Community Health Unit*

British Society of Paedadontic Dentists

Professor C G D Brook, Professor of Paediatric Endocrinology, *University College London Medical School*

Ms Jill Brownson, Chairman, *Association of Paediatric Chartered Physiotherapists*

Ms Sue Burr, Advisor, Paediatric Nursing, *Royal College of Nursing*

Ms Margaret A Buttigeig, Director, *Health Visitors Association*

Dr Jill Carlisle, Medical Advisor to the *British Dyslexia Association*

Mr Adrian Chubb, Chief Executive, *Nottingham Community Health NHS Trust*

Community Hygiene Concern

P Curry, School Health Advisor, *South Warwickshire*

Dr J S Davis, Consultant Community Paediatrician, Dewsbury *Healthcare NHS Trust*

Dr J M Donnelly, Consultant Community Paediatrician, Aylesbury *Vale Community Healthcare NHS Trust*

Dr E H Dryburgh, Consultant Community Paediatrician, North *West Anglia Healthcare Trust*

Dr David Elliman, Consultant in Community Child Health, *St George's Health care NHS Trust*

Ms D Fitton, School Nurse Manager, *St Georges London*

Dr Aileen Fogerty, SCMO, *Northampton General Hospital NHS Trust*

Mrs E H Fradd, Senior Nurse Manager, Children's Services, *Queens Medical Centre, Nottingham*

Dr Anne Franklin, *Chelmsford*

Mr Tam Fry, Honorary Chairman, *Child Growth Foundation*

Dr Peter A Garder, for *The Society of Public Health*

Dr Penny Gibson, Consultant Community Paediatrician *The Jarvis Centre, North Downs Community Health Unit*

Ms Pippa Gough, Professional Officer, Health Visiting & Community Nursing, *United Kingdom Central Council for Nursing, Midwifery and Health Visiting*

Dr S H Green, Secretary, *British Paediatric Neurology Association*

Dr Helen Grindulis, Consultant Community Paediatrician, *Sandwell Hospitals* and *Community Health Service*

Dr Shirley M Gumpel, SCMO, Audiology, *St Mary's Hospital, Paddington Green Children's Unit*

Professor D M B Hall, *University* of *Sheffield*

Ms M D Hall, *College of Occupational Physiotherapists*

Dr Roger Harrington, *Medical Officers of Schools Association*

Mrs L Harris *Essex and Herts School Nurses*

Professor D J Hatch, *The Association of Paediatric Anaesthetists*

Health Education Authority

Dr P C Hindmarsh, Senior Lecturer in Paediatric Endocrinology, for *British Society for Paediatric Endocrinology*

Ms Rachael Hodgkin, *Principal Policy Officer, National Children's Bureau*

Dr Anita Hooper, senior medical officer (school health), Greenwork healthcare

Professor Ieuan A Hughes, Department of Paediatrics, *Addenbrooke's Hospital, Cambridge*

Mr Tim Hughes. for *The Anaphylaxis Campaign*

Richard James, Chief Executive, *Severn NHS Trust*

Dr C Jenkins, SCMO, *Powys Healthcare NHS Trust*

Dr D I Johnston, Consultant Paediatrician, *Queens Medical Centre, Nottingham*

Dr Isabel Jones, Consultant Community Paediatrician, *Mid Sussex NHS Trust*

Dr Y S Kaplan, SCMO, *Rotherham Priority NHS Trust*

Dr H H Kaye, Consultant Paediatrician, Clinical Head of Services, *Child Health, Scarborough & North East Yorkshire Healthcare*

Ros Kenton, Director of Operations, *North Warwickshire NHS Trust*

Dr G D Kewley, Consultant Paediatrician, *Crawley and Redhill Hospitals*

Dr E Knight-Jones, Consultant in Developmental Paediatrics and Childhood Handicap, *Children's Community Health Services Nottingham Health NHS Trust*

Dr Sebastian Kraemer, Consultant Psychiatrist, *Child s Family Psychiatric Service, London, N6*

Dr M G Lane, Clinical Medical Officer, *Farnham*

Dr Sara Levene, medical consultant, *Child Accident Prevention Trust*

Dr M J Lowe, Deputy Secretary, *British Medical Association*

Dr Alexander Macrea, Consultant Community Paediatrician, *Royal Berkshire and Battle Hospitals NHS Trust*

Dr C McCowen, Clinical Director, Family Health, *North Tees General Hospital, Stockton on Tees*

Ms F McElderry, *National Association of Paediatric Occupational Therapists*

Dr P P Mycock, Consultant Community Paediatrician, *Child Development Unit, Stepping Hill Hospital, Stockport*

Dr T M Myint, PMO, *Primary Care Directorate, Dewsbury Health Care NHS Trust*

Ms E M Nair, Director, Nursing and Consumer Affairs, *Northern Health & Social Services Board, Ballymena*

National Association for all Heads and Deputies

Ms Linda Neal, School Nurse, *St Georges Healthcare NHS Trust*

Dr Chris Newman, Director, Paediatric Business Unit, *Royal Berkshire & Battle Hospitals NHS Trust*

Dr J R Owens, Clinical Director, Family Health Services Directorate, *East Cheshire NHS Trust*

Dr Jill Painter, SCMO, *Mancunian Community Health NHS Trust*

Professor John Pearce, Professor of Child & Adolescent Psychiatry, *University* of *Nottingham*

Peterborough, Senior Clinical Medical Officers

Mrs L M Pinson, Dental Services Manager, *Northern Birmingham Community NHS Trust*

Dr Bill Reith, *Royal College of General Practitioners*

F A Rice, Director Hun an Resources, Nursing, *Southern Health and Social Services Board, Craigavon*

David Rivett, UK Co-ordinator, European Network of Health Promoting Schools, *Health Education Authority*

Dr Graham Roberts, Reader in Paediatric Dentistry, *Institute of Child Health, London*

Mrs Kit Sampson, former Gypsy Liaison Officer, *East Anglian Regional Health Authority*

Dr Anna Sharma, SCMO, *Camden & Islington Community Health Services NHS Trust*

Dr J E Shorland, Consultant Community Paediatrician, *Rotherham Priority Health Trust*

Dr V A Shrubb, Consultant Community Paediatrician, *Southampton Community Child Health Services*

Dr D A Slevin, Chief Executive, *The National Board for Nursing, Midwifery and Health Visiting for Northern Ireland*

Dr C A Smalley, for *Wessex Community Paediatricians*

Ms G I Smythe, Nursing Officer, *Department of Health and Social Services, Belfast*

D D Smythe, General *Manager, Northern Health and Social Services Board, Balymena*

Dr David Sowden, *Royal College of General Practitioners*

Ms Lorna Spenceley, Information Services Manager, *AFASIC*

Dr A Stanton, Consultant Community Paediatrician, *Solihull Healthcare*

Ms Kirsteen Tait, Director, *National Association for the Education of Sick Children*

Dr A Tandy, Consultant Community Paediatrician, *Taunton*

Professor Brent Taylor, *Royal Free Hampstead NHS Trust*

Dr A M Telford, Director of Public Health, *Southern Health & Social Services Board*

Lynette Thomas, Chairman, *Amalgamated Association of School Nurses*

Dr R H Todman, *Lancashire Community Paediatricians*

Ms Susan Twemlow, Specialist Services *Manager, Central Nottinghamshire Healthcare NHS Trust*

Dr Peter Z A Vermaak, Consultant Paediatrician, *Gwent*

Dr David Vickers, *Lifespan Healthcare, Cambridge*

Joanna Vinceny, *Eating Disorders Association*

Mrs M C Waddell, Director of *Nursing, Eastern Health & Social Services Board, Belfast*

Dr Tony Waterston, British Association for Community Child Health

Dr J D Williamson, Director of Public Health, *Kingston S Richmond*

Mrs N M Williamson, Acting Family Services Manager, *Andover District Community Healthcare NHS Trust*

Dr Sara Young, Lead SCMO, (Child Health), *East Yorkshire Community Healthcare*

Acknowledgements

My thanks to the members of the working party and all those who submitted evidence or commented on the consultant document. Special thanks to Maureen Robinson, BPA secretariat for keeping the working party on the road and Sam Lingam-BPA honorary assistant editor for design and help with the production of the publication.

Index

Clumsy children 42
Collaboration 94
  accident prevention 41
  adolescent health 59
  child protection 78
  children *looked after* 81
  core programme for schools 44
  disability 65
  disadvantaged children 87
  emotional/ behavioural problems 71
  health promotion 37
  health services 23
  infection control 55
Colour vision testing 46, 49-50
Combined child health service 14
Communicable diseases 54-57
Community changes 12
Community paediatric team 31
Community paediatricians 33
Community paediatrics 73-75
  management 17
  research 17
  training 15-16
  see also Health services for school age
    children
Confidentiality 22
Consent
  children *looked after* 81
  parental 21-22, 23
Constitutional delay in growth and
    puberty (CDGP) 48
Consultant led community paediatric
    service 15-16
Consultants in communicable disease
    control (CCDC) 54, 55, 56
Continuing medical education (CME) 16
Continuity of care 67, 68
  children *looked after* 82
  disadvantaged children 87, 88
Control of substances hazardous to health
    (COSHH) regulations (1988) 55
Core programme for schools 42-52, 91

Core surveillance programmes 25
Coronary heart disease 6, 13, 35-36
Court Report (1976) 1, 15, 31
Critical illness 75-76
Culture 12
  inter-country adoption 84
  see also Ethnic minorities
Cycles of disadvantage 80

D

Data collection *see* Information
Definitions 3 Delinquency 69
Dental health 13, 53-54, 92
Depression 59, 69
Developmental problems 63-69, 92
Disability 6, 63-73
  adolescents 58
  behavioural problems *see* Behavioural
    problems
  developmental problems 63-73
  emotional problems *see* Emotional
    problems
  legislation 63
  prevalence 13
  register 65
  special needs *see* Special needs children
Disabled Persons Act (1986) 67
Disadvantage 84-89, 93
District consortia 2, 94
District factfiles 91
District health authorities 5
District immunisation co-ordinators 55
Divorce rate 11
Drop in clinics 60
Drug misuse 57

E

Education Act (1907) 5
Education Act (1944) 5
Education Act (1981) 5